CONTENTS

CONDUCT OF MONETARY POLICY

Report of the Federal Reserve Board pursuant to the Full Employment and Balanced Growth Act of 1978, P.L. 95–523 and The State of the Economy

HEARING

BEFORE THE

SUBCOMMITTEE ON ECONOMIC GROWTH AND CREDIT FORMATION

OF THE

COMMITTEE ON BANKING, FINANCE AND URBAN AFFAIRS

HOUSE OF REPRESENTATIVES

ONE HUNDRED THIRD CONGRESS

SECOND SESSION

JULY 22, 1994

Printed for the use of the Committee on Banking, Finance and Urban Affairs

Serial No. 103–155

U.S. GOVERNMENT PRINTING OFFICE

81–438 CC WASHINGTON : 1994

For sale by the U.S. Government Printing Office
Superintendent of Documents, Congressional Sales Office, Washington, DC 20402
ISBN 0-16-045885-4

HOUSE COMMITTEE ON BANKING, FINANCE AND URBAN AFFAIRS

HENRY B. GONZALEZ, Texas, *Chairman*

STEPHEN L. NEAL, North Carolina
JOHN J. LAFALCE, New York
BRUCE F. VENTO, Minnesota
CHARLES E. SCHUMER, New York
BARNEY FRANK, Massachusetts
PAUL E. KANJORSKI, Pennsylvania
JOSEPH P. KENNEDY II, Massachusetts
FLOYD H. FLAKE, New York
KWEISI MFUME, Maryland
MAXINE WATERS, California
LARRY LAROCCO, Idaho
BILL ORTON, Utah
JIM BACCHUS, Florida
HERBERT C. KLEIN, New Jersey
CAROLYN B. MALONEY, New York
PETER DEUTSCH, Florida
LUIS V. GUTIERREZ, Illinois
BOBBY L. RUSH, Illinois
LUCILLE ROYBAL-ALLARD, California
THOMAS M. BARRETT, Wisconsin
ELIZABETH FURSE, Oregon
NYDIA M. VELAZQUEZ, New York
ALBERT R. WYNN, Maryland
CLEO FIELDS, Louisiana
MELVIN WATT, North Carolina
MAURICE HINCHEY, New York
CALVIN M. DOOLEY, California
RON KLINK, Pennsylvania
ERIC FINGERHUT, Ohio

JAMES A. LEACH, Iowa
BILL McCOLLUM, Florida
MARGE ROUKEMA, New Jersey
DOUG BEREUTER, Nebraska
THOMAS J. RIDGE, Pennsylvania
TOBY ROTH, Wisconsin
ALFRED A. (AL) McCANDLESS, California
RICHARD H. BAKER, Louisiana
JIM NUSSLE, Iowa
CRAIG THOMAS, Wyoming
SAM JOHNSON, Texas
DEBORAH PRYCE, Ohio
JOHN LINDER, Georgia
JOE KNOLLENBERG, Michigan
RICK LAZIO, New York
ROD GRAMS, Minnesota
SPENCER BACHUS, Alabama
MIKE HUFFINGTON, California
MICHAEL CASTLE, Delaware
PETER KING, New York

BERNARD SANDERS, Vermont

SUBCOMMITTEE ON ECONOMIC GROWTH AND CREDIT FORMATION

PAUL E. KANJORSKI, Pennsylvania, *Chairman*

STEPHEN L. NEAL, North Carolina
JOHN J. LAFALCE, New York
BILL ORTON, Utah
HERBERT C. KLEIN, New Jersey
NYDIA M. VELAZQUEZ, New York
CALVIN M. DOOLEY, California
RON KLINK, Pennsylvania
ERIC FINGERHUT, Ohio

THOMAS J. RIDGE, Pennsylvania
BILL McCOLLUM, Florida
TOBY ROTH, Wisconsin
JIM NUSSLE, Iowa
MARGE ROUKEMA, New Jersey
PETER KING, New York

CONDUCT OF MONETARY POLICY

FRIDAY, JULY 22, 1994

HOUSE OF REPRESENTATIVES,
SUBCOMMITTEE ON ECONOMIC GROWTH AND
CREDIT FORMATION,
COMMITTEE ON BANKING, FINANCE AND URBAN AFFAIRS,
Washington, DC.

The subcommittee met, pursuant to notice, at 10 a.m., in room 340, Cannon House Office Building, Hon. Paul E. Kanjorski [chairman of the subcommittee] presiding.

Present: Chairman Kanjorski, Representatives Neal, Orton, Klein, Dooley, Klink, Fingerhut, Roth, and Nussle.

Also present: Representative Leach.

Chairman KANJORSKI. The subcommittee will come to order.

The subcommittee meets today to receive the biennial report of the Board of Governors of the Federal Reserve System on the conduct of the monetary policy and the state of the economy as mandated in the Full Employment Balanced Growth Act of 1978.

Under President Clinton, the Nation's economy has undergone a significant recovery and growth since emerging from the recession in the early 1990's. Our gross national product has increased at a healthy rate, but unemployment rates continue to decline and inflation remains at a low level.

Mr. Chairman, we will have other members of the subcommittee join us today and I am sure some of them will ask you to play the role of prognosticator, as you tend to do very well. I suspect that in the 10 years that I have been in Congress we probably have had better cooperation between the Federal Reserve and the Office of the President in attempting to resolve budget problems and the economy and improve the economy than we have had in a long time.

So this subcommittee appreciates that effort on your part and, of course, recognizes the fact that the administration is different from the standpoint of political persuasion of the last administration and it obviously indicates that America is capable in this very tough time to have a bipartisan economic policy that is successful.

To that end, I congratulate you and I think that you deserve merit and recognition for the Federal Reserve portion of what we can attribute to the American recovery. I am a little disturbed and, unfortunately, the American people and the business community of America haven't quite recognized the importance of the accomplishments of the Clinton administration economically, and particularly as you have stated in your prior testimony, the major accomplishment of the balanced budget process that we went through last year or the attempt to decrease the deficit significantly that we went through last year.

It is well on track, as I gather. It is more optimistic than any of us would imagine. We have got work to do and we look forward to your recommendations on that point.

On the other hand, during the questioning today I would like you to give some thought later on, perhaps we could discuss it, I am a little bit—still interested in the Bank of International Settlements and I have given it some thought. We have not had a chance to discuss it personally in the intervening weeks since we originally discussed that, but I have some thought processes that both myself and the subcommittee probably needs the ability to get the best economic and constitutional minds in the country to give us some advice on that area and perhaps discuss some format that you would think would be relatively worthwhile to pursue along that end.

Senator Gore, when he was a Senator, before he was Vice President, used to say the wrong things are up and the wrong things are down and suddenly July 1994 you have seen a significant change of the wrong things being up and the wrong things being down and now we see the right things being up and the right things being down.

We would like some anticipation from you what we could expect over the next year or 2 years and whether or not it is your opinion the recovery is sufficiently supported and on a strong enough foundation that we can look at the rest of the 1990's to encourage the American business community to become as competitive as we know they can be in the world market for the remainder of the 20th century.

So I thank you for your presence today and I would be happy to recognize my colleague from Iowa.

Mr. LEACH. Thank you, Mr. Chairman. I have no opening comment.

Chairman KANJORSKI. And the gentleman from Utah.

Mr. ORTON. I would just like to welcome the Chairman here and look forward to your statement.

Mr. GREENSPAN. Thank you.

Chairman KANJORSKI. Mr. Chairman, you may proceed.

STATEMENT OF ALAN GREENSPAN, CHAIRMAN, BOARD OF GOVERNORS OF THE FEDERAL RESERVE SYSTEM

Mr. GREENSPAN. Thank you very much, gentlemen.

It is a pleasure to appear before this subcommittee to discuss with you recent economic developments and the Federal Reserve's conduct of monetary policy.

The favorable performance of the economy continued in the first half of 1994. Economic growth was strong, unemployment fell appreciably, and inflation remained subdued. To sustain the expansion, the Federal Reserve adjusted monetary policy over recent months so as to contain potential inflation pressures.

Our actions this year can be understood by reference to policy under the previous several years. Through that period, the Federal Reserve moved toward and then maintained for a considerable time a purposefully accomodative stance of policy. During 1993, that stance was associated with low levels of real short-term interest rates—around zero. We judged that low interest rates would be necessary for a time to overcome the effects of a number of factors that were restraining the economic expansion, including heavy debt burdens of households and businesses and tighter credit policies of many lenders.

By early this year, however, it became clear that many of these impediments had diminished and that the economy had consequently gained considerable momentum. In these circumstances, it was no longer appropriate to maintain an accomodative policy. Indeed, history strongly suggests that maintenance of real short-term rates at levels prevailing last year ultimately would have fueled inflationary pressures and imbalances.

Accordingly, the Federal Open Market Committee at its meeting in early February decided to move away from its accommodative posture by tightening reserve market conditions. Given the level of real short-term rates and the evident momentum in the economy, it seemed likely that a substantial cumulative adjustment of policy would be needed. However, committee members recognized that financial markets were not fully prepared for this action. Many were concerned that a marked shift in the stance of policy, while necessary, could precipitate an exaggerated reaction in financial markets.

With this in mind, we initially tightened reserve conditions only slightly, just enough to raise the Federal funds rate a quarter of a percentage point. And the financial markets did indeed react sharply, with substantial increases in longer term interest rates and declines in stock prices. Markets remained unsettled for several months and we continued to move cautiously in March and April in the process of moving away from our accommodative stance. By mid-May, however, a considerable portion of the adjustment in portfolios to the new rate environment appeared to have taken place. With financial markets evidently better prepared to absorb a larger move, the Federal Reserve could substantially complete the removal of the degree of monetary accommodation that prevailed throughout 1993.

The Board raised the discount rate a half a percentage point, a move that was fully passed through to reserve market conditions by the FOMC. Partly to minimize any market confusion about the extent of and rationale for our moves, the Federal Reserve has announced each action and in relevant instances, provided an explanation. At its meeting in early July, the FOMC faced considerable uncertainty about the pace of expansion and pressures on prices going forward. And it made no further adjustment in its policy stance.

Nonetheless, it is an open question whether our actions to date have been sufficient to head off inflationary pressures and thus maintain favorable trends in the economy. Labor demand has been quite strong, pointing to robust growth in production and incomes. To be sure, some hints of moderation in the growth of the domestic final demand have appeared, and the recent indications of accelerating inventory accumulation may suggest an unwanted backing up of stocks. Conversely, the inventory accumulation may reflect pressures on firms who had brought inventories down to suboptimal levels and now need to replenish them. In the latter case, stock-building may continue at an above-normal rate supporting production for quite some time. Moreover, the improving economic conditions of our trading partners should add impetus to aggregate demand from the external sector.

How these forces balance out in the coming months could be critical in determining whether inflation will remain in check, for the amount of slack in the economy, while difficult to judge, appears to have become relatively small. An increase of inflation would come at considerable cost. We would lose hard-won ground in the fight against inflation expectations, ground that would be difficult to recapture later; our long-run economic performance would be impaired by the inefficiencies associated with higher inflation if it persisted, and harsher policy actions would eventually be necessary to reverse the upsurge in inflationary instabilities. We are determined to prevent such an outcome and currently are monitoring economic and financial data carefully to assess whether additional adjustments are appropriate.

The economic figures that have formed the backdrop of our policy actions so far this year confirm that a rapid expansion has been in progress. Following growth at an annual rate of 7 percent in the fourth quarter of last year, real gross domestic product rose at nearly a 3.5 percent rate during the first quarter. A conceptually equivalent measure of aggregate output, gross domestic income, exhibited even larger gains in the fourth and first quarters. At this stage, available data leave some uncertainty regarding the pace of economic activity over the past 3 months. Nonetheless, the evidence in hand makes it reasonably clear that growth remained appreciably above its longer run trend. The robust expansion over the first half of 1994 has been reflected in substantial increases in employment.

The accumulating evidence of stronger than expected economic growth here and abroad, combined with changing expectations of policy actions by the Federal Reserve, as well as other central banks, prompted considerable increases in long-term interest rates in occasionally volatile markets over the first half of the year.

The recent weakness in bond prices was not limited to the United States, but was accompanied by a surge in foreign interest rates.

Rising foreign interest rates, concerns in markets about the prospects for reduced trade tensions and about U.S. inflation contributed to considerable activity directed at rebalancing international investment portfolios. One effect of this activity appears to have been a substantial decline of the foreign exchange value of the dollar on net over the past 6 months. Foreign exchange rates are key prices in the American economy with significant implications for the volumes of exports and imports as well as the prices of imports and domestically produced items that compete with imports. The foreign exchange value of the dollar can also provide useful insights into inflation expectations. If we conduct an appropriate monetary policy—and appropriate economic policies more generally—we shall achieve our goals of solid economic growth and price stability and such economic results will ensure that dollar-denominated assets remain attractive to global investors, which is essential to the dollar's continuing role as the world's principal reserve currency.

Rising interest rates have contributed to another substantial gain in the velocity of the broad monetary aggregates this year. As a consequence, growth of both aggregates near the lower ends of the 1994 ranges is considered to be consistent with achieving our objectives for economic performance, and the ranges were left unchanged.

The committee also decided, on a provisional basis, to carry forward the current ranges of the monetary aggregates of 1995.

Regarding domestic nonfinancial sector debt, we made no adjustment to this year's monitoring range, but elected to set a provisional monitoring range for 1995 of 3 to 7 percent, a percentage point lower than last year's. A lower range would conform with some deceleration in nominal income, in the process of containing inflation and ultimately making progress toward price stability.

With appropriate monetary policies, the Board members and the Reserve Bank presidents see the economy settling into more moderate rates of growth over the next six quarters and inflation remaining relatively subdued.

In view of rapid economic growth recently and narrowing margins of slack in productive capacity, there has been considerable interest of late in the Federal Reserve's ideas about the longrun trends in output and employment consistent with avoiding pressures on prices. My colleagues and I don't think the numerical estimates of these trends by the FOMC would be useful in helping Congress and the public gauge our policy strategy. We believe, instead, that our intentions are best conveyed in terms of our declared objective of fostering as much growth of the output and employment as can be achieved without placing destabilizing inflationary pressures on productive resources. There is considerable uncertainty about what that goal implies for the expansion of gross domestic product and rates of unemployment at the economy's full potential.

Uncertainties around these variables arise because identifying economic relationships is always difficult, partly owing to limitations of the data. But more fundamentally, all policymakers recognize that notions of potential GDP growth and the so-called natural rate of unemployment are considerable simplifications, useful in conceptual models but subject to a variety of real world complications. Our economy is a complex, dynamic system, comprising countless and diverse households, services, products, and prices, interacting in a multitude of markets. Estimates of macroeconomic relationships, as best we can make them, are useful starting points for analysis, but they are just starting points.

Given questions about the aggregate relationships, policymakers need to look below the surface into the markets themselves for evidence of tightness that might indicate whether inflationary pressures are indeed building.

If the economy were nearing capacity, we would expect to see certain patterns in the statistical and anecdotal information. With increasing frequency and intensity, reports of shortages of skilled labor, strikes, and instances of difficulties in finding workers in specific regions, for example, all would be more likely. Businesses might have difficulty obtaining certain materials and the price of these materials would rise.

In recent months we have seen some of these signs. There are reports of shortages of some types of labor: Construction workers and truck drivers, for instance. Indexes of vendor performance have deteriorated considerably, and manufacturers are paying higher prices for materials used in their production processes. As yet, these sorts of indications do not seem to be widespread across the economy. Nonetheless, we shall need to be particularly alert to these emerging signs in considering further adjustments to policy in the period ahead.

In light of the uncertainties about aggregate measures of economic potential, the Federal Reserve cannot rely heavily on any one estimate of either the natural rate of unemployment, as it is called, or potential GDP growth. Most important, we have no intention of setting artificial limits on employment or growth.

A more significant issue for economic policymakers than the precise values of such estimates is what can be done to maximize sustainable employment and economic growth. We need, for example, to give careful attention to the problem of unemployment as noted by the G–7 leaders at their recent summit. We could raise output and living standards around the world and at the same time ease many social problems if more people were working.

We ought to be encouraging measures to increase the flexibility of our work force and labor markets. Improving education and training and facilitating better and more rapid matching of workers with jobs are essential elements in making more effective use of the American workers.

Congress and the administration also can continue to contribute to the growth of our economy's capital and productivity through a sound fiscal policy. The extension of the spending caps in last year's budget agreements was a significant step in putting fiscal policy on a more sustainable longrun path. But under current law, the deficit as a percent of GDP will begin to expand again as we move into the next century with unacceptable consequences for financial stability and economic growth. Only by reducing the growth in spending is ultimate balance achievable.

As I have emphasized many times, Mr. Chairman, the Federal Reserve also can contribute to the achievement of our overriding goal—maximum sustainable economic growth—by pursuing and ultimately achieving a stable price level.

There is some evidence to suggest that the stronger trend of productivity growth we have witnessed over the recent past is due at least partly to the beneficial effects of low rates of inflation.

Our Nation has made considerable progress in putting the economy on a sound footing in the past few years. To preserve and extend these advances, our monetary and fiscal policies will need to remain disciplined and focused on our long-term objectives. We would be foolish to squander our recent gains for near-term benefits that would prove ephemeral. Indeed, by fostering progress toward price stability, achieving lower Federal budget deficits, and encouraging competitive markets both here and abroad, we will help ensure the continued vitality of our Nation's economy now and for many years into the future.

Mr. Chairman, as I am sure you have noted, I have excerpted quite considerably from my prepared text and request my full remarks be included for the record.

[The prepared statement of Mr. Greenspan can be found in the appendix.]

Chairman KANJORSKI. Without objection, so ordered.

Thank you very much, Mr. Chairman. Mr. Chairman, you referred in your closing remarks in the statement to the fact that we have to get a handle even further on the budget deficit if we are to have expanded, continued growth in the economy in the years ahead. Do you have a preference?

Does it matter if the policy of the Congress and government is in terms of whether we are spending money in consumption or investment? Is there a need for us to evaluate the quality of government expenditures over the next several years that would have a major impact on where the American economy was going?

Mr. GREENSPAN. Mr. Chairman, obviously, it does matter what we spend it on and clearly investment-type outlays have a more important positive effect and less of a negative effect than strictly consumption. But I would be hesitant to conclude from that that we move toward a capital budget as distinct from our simple unified budget.

And the reason is that while, from analytical and public policy points of view, it is important to distinguish whether or not the types of outlays that we are expending are consumption-rated or investment-rated, at the end of the day, all differences between receipts and outlays of all types have to be funded by the sale of Federal obligations in the markets. And the markets cannot distinguish in the intermediate period whether the financing is for investment or whether it is for consumption. History suggests to us that we have to be very careful in this area, and I suggest that while we should look at the composition of what we spend, we should be very careful not to veer away from the unified budget in our projections into the future, because the financial markets around the world, all of the individuals who hold dollar-denominated assets, look, as best as I can judge, at the financing requirements of the U.S. Treasury and are not focused very much on the composition of what those expenditures are which led to it. And, therefore, the presumption that somehow deficit spending on consumption items alone is really all that the markets would look at is surely not the case, at least history clearly indicates that it has not been the case.

Chairman KANJORSKI. Mr. Chairman, at the conclusion of the falling dollar, do you have any observations for the American people as to what we can expect and anticipate as our over-adjustment, as a matter of fact, is in fact a reflection of the fundamental weaknesses of the currency?

Mr. GREENSPAN. Mr. Chairman, I have been disinclined to try to forecast what the dollar will or will not do at any particular point in time. It is obviously a very complex issue and all I can say is I would reiterate basically what Under Secretary Summers said yesterday before the Senate Banking Committee about the nature of forces which are driving the dollar.

Clearly, it is in our interest to have a stronger dollar. It is in our interest because we are the reserve currency in the world, particularly, and as you may note what I indicated in my prepared remarks, there are technical issues with respect to the effect of the falling dollar on inflation and that clearly is adverse. But it is very important that the U.S. Government in all its areas and aspects recognize, as indeed Secretary Bentsen's and Under Secretary Summers' comments in recent days have indicated that a stronger dollar essentially helps the United States and indeed helps our trading partners as best we can judge.

Chairman KANJORSKI. I guess one last question in that regard, have the foreign central banks contacted or coordinated with the Fed regarding purchase of dollars? Have you had any cooperation using the Federal Reserve with the foreign central banks?

Mr. GREENSPAN. We talk to them all the time. Indeed, we have been embarked upon numerous coordinated interventions in the international financial currency markets over the years and this results from a fairly close relationship that exists among the major central banks in the world. I speak to my colleagues quite often trying to get a sense from them as to what is happening in Europe and Japan and elsewhere.

And since we are in a global economy, the presumption that the United States somehow can exist as an independent entity from the rest of the world—a notion which may have had some validity 40 years ago—is increasingly less apparent today and it is quite important for us to make certain that we coordinate as best we can with our colleagues.

Chairman KANJORSKI. Mr. Roth.

Mr. ROTH. Thank you, Mr. Chairman.

Chairman Greenspan, it is nice to have you with us again.

Mr. GREENSPAN. Thank you very much.

Mr. ROTH. Mr. Chairman, the last time that we were together, I think we basically came down to a form—at least I did, right or wrongly—that as inflation goes up, interest rates go up. Inflation stabilized, interest rates will stabilize. Is that still pretty well the formula that we have today?

Mr. GREENSPAN. There is no question that a significant part of the level of interest rates, both short and long, reflect inflation expectations. Now, inflation expectations, remember, are not the same thing as inflation. These are expectations of players in the market of what they think inflation is going to be. They could be wrong, but nonetheless that is what sets those particular relationships. So very clearly we see that inflation is a factor.

We also have to remember that there are other elements which move real interest rates, those already adjusted for inflation. And that largely is a consequence of the changes in the underlying supply and demand for credit in the international markets of capital and savings. Some interest rates levels reflect that and so I would say inflation expectations are very important elements, in certain instances overriding elements, in the level of interest rates but not the only element.

Mr. ROTH. What significance do you attach to the recent slowdown of single-family housing starts in America?

Mr. GREENSPAN. We saw a really quite extraordinary rise as mortgage interest rates fell and affordability improved very measurably in a period when there was a significant backlog of demand for single-family residences. We had an extraordinary period of very strong demand and, of course, we even had a very strong demand for existing homes which turned over quite significantly during the period.

Partly because we have gone through part of the backlog, partly because mortgage interest rates have turned back up, we are getting a somewhat slower pace of single-family residences and the data that we are looking at with respect to home sales, permits, and starts are all consistent with that view of gradual coming off the peaks that we experienced last year.

Mr. ROTH. So you feel that we are slowing down somewhat, as I interpret what you are saying. You don't expect it to go back up again. We are sort of leveling off now at a lower rate, is that what you are saying?

Mr. GREENSPAN. I really don't know, and I don't want to comment, because it is going to depend on a number of other things, but what I am reasonably sure of is it is not going to go straight down. There is no evidence of that. The demand is still strong. Even though mortgage interest rates have gone up, by historical standards they remain quite low and the affordability of houses is really quite solid.

Mr. ROTH. Mr. Chairman, here on Capitol Hill, you know, we are really wrestling with an issue on health care and one of the key elements in that, of course, is employer mandates. Now, we have had all kinds of testimony on both sides, people saying you impose an employer mandate, you are going to lose a lot of jobs in America. Other people say you have to have employer mandates to pay for health care.

What is your opinion? Do you think if we had employer mandates that it would impact on our economy negatively?

Mr. GREENSPAN. Congressman, I very purposefully stayed away from trying to get involved in the details of——

Mr. ROTH. I am trying to get you involved because I want you to help me make up my mind.

Mr. GREENSPAN. All I can say, Congressman, is to date I have been rather successful in being rather evasive on this issue, and I have learned how to do it with a great degree of skill.

Mr. ROTH. That is true.

Mr. GREENSPAN. In all seriousness, though, the central bank's real interest is the bottom line. All we are fundamentally interested in is the issue of what are the volume requirements of the U.S. Treasury because as a central bank our policies are crucially involved with that. So we have stayed away from the issue of evaluating or giving our comments on the nature of the composition of receipts and expenditures.

Mr. ROTH. I just had one more question because I want to limit my time—we have a lot of other Congressmen here that want to ask questions this morning—and that deals with Social Security and the chairman asked a question before about the deficit and so on. Last year we had some $53 billion in surplus in Social Security which was used by the government for other purposes. Now, senior citizens around the country are very upset because they feel all this surplus money went out and put IOUs into their fund and that is it. What they would like to see is this money invested for Social Security other than giving it to the government in the form of IOUs. What is your opinion about that?

Mr. GREENSPAN. As you know, Congressman, this issue has come up over decades and, indeed, I recall when I was involved with the Social Security Commission over a decade ago, we went through that issue in some detail. It is a very complex question and the only thing that I would say in this regard, which is not really addressing the question you raise which is a very important question, is that one must be careful not to view the Social Security surpluses off budget.

In other words, I know that the statute says you do it that way. But from an economic point of view, it is important to stay with the unified budget concept if we are going to get the appropriate measure of how the Federal Government's budget impacts our economy.

Mr. ROTH. Thank you, Mr. Chairman.

Chairman KANJORSKI. Mr. Klink.

Mr. KLINK. Thank you very much, Chairman Greenspan. It is nice to have you with us.

I wanted to just touch on one point that you made toward the end of your speech. You were talking about the fact of deficit reduction has been very timely, the Federal Government's deficit reduction. Can I get you to expand upon that a little bit and talk more because, as you know, we had a discussion yesterday and some votes on the floor on entitlement caps. I am not sure if what we do and what you do is an exact science or not. The question is——

Mr. GREENSPAN. I can't speak for your——

Mr. KLINK. How fast do we do this. I mean what are the ramifications of imposing even tighter caps on discretionary spending and tightening the caps on the entitlements? Where are we heading and how does that help you do your job?

Mr. GREENSPAN. Congressman, as I indicated in my prepared remarks, and I believe my colleagues would agree with this, the extension and the enforcement of the spending caps, in this case discretionary, have really been quite a surprise. Because when they were initially put in place, as you may recall, it was quite feasible to presume that either the President would declare that certain expenditures were an emergency, because that word could be used very loosely, or at the extreme, that it would only require a majority of both Houses to break the caps.

In the event, and I think this is a very important issue which is very positive for the future, it has been politically extraordinarily difficult to do either and I interpret that as meaning that the American people have increasingly become aware of the significant problems which the chronic long-term budget deficit can have on our economy in the short term, but just as importantly for the next generation, and the notion that caps are working and that they are feasible is the best fiscal policy surprise that we have all had. The administration and the Congress should be congratulated for pressing this type of structure forward because you would know far better than I how many motions and bills die because they didn't meet the caps or they couldn't find pay-go offsets.

And that more than anything has been a very crucial factor in bringing the budget deficit down and if we can resolve the long-term budget problem, after all of these decades, we could find that we will have a materially positive effect on the financing of our budget and a major reduction in the drain on what I would call a meager saving flow in the United States.

So ideally, I would even argue that we should move toward a budget surplus and contribute to national saving because of the particular problems that we have. I discussed this at some length in my prepared remarks and I don't want to get into it here, but on the issue of the caps on entitlements per se, I haven't come to a conclusion because I haven't had a chance to look at the approach of the legislation that is in the bill.

Mr. KLINK. The thing that we wrestle with here obviously as you mentioned that bills that die because you can't find offsets. When we are spending less, there are certain segments of our manufacturing where the government is a purchaser that is adversely affected and some of that is manufacturing that is very important to our Nation because it may be defense-related, it may have some other specific need. Is that of concern to you that there will be segments of our manufacturing that would be left behind as we become more fiscally responsible?

Mr. GREENSPAN. It is not so much that we would become more fiscally responsible because in the longer run there is nothing that helps American manufacturing and competitiveness better than having a noninflationary environment and a noninflationary environment is very significantly fostered by budget discipline.

So while I have no doubt that when you change the composition of the types of procurement that are involved in our manfacturing sector from defense to nondefense, or within the defense area where there has been a tremendous shuffle—that is something that has been going on for decades—some individual institutions, manufacturing firms, and companies have prospered. Others have faded away or shrunk to negligible proportions. I see no reason to suspect that that process will not continue.

It is important to recognize that one of the great strengths of the American economy is the dynamism, the churning that is going on all the time for competitive reasons and the impact of that is to make a very substantial positive contribution to productivity and economic growth.

I like to cite the figure, for example, Congressman, that there are 300,000 people a week who lose their jobs but a substantially larger number now who are getting jobs, so it is a very big turnover. This is much larger than in Europe and I believe in Japan. And it is one of our really major strengths. So I see no alternative to allowing that process to happen. While I recognize it requires some adjustments in a lot of companies, these are basically the mechanisms which produce higher standards of living.

Mr. KLINK. Thank you, Chairman.

Chairman KANJORSKI. Thank you very much, Mr. Klink.

Mr. Leach.

Mr. LEACH. Thank you, Mr. Chairman. Well, I would like, Mr. Chairman, to return for a minute to the foreign currency issue.

I, personally, thoroughly agree with that, that a stronger dollar is in the country's best interest at this time. Where I have some differentiation judgment, though, is on this issue of free market versus government intervention. And it strikes me that the administration is sending some signals over the past year that they could accept a weaker dollar and based upon perhaps some misreading of judgment or misreading of this circumstance, the government has chosen to indicate that that isn't the policy and so in essence has taken resources that are public and put them at risk; that is, it has intervened in the markets.

If the markets go the right direction, the taxpayer ends up, just as one plays the commodities market, with a profit. If they go the wrong way, the reverse. But here, I mean one of the great changes over the last several decades has been that reserves of governments are much less in relationship to the size of the market and every day they are getting smaller and smaller.

In fact, one set of calculations, although it is an exaggerated set because it isn't just the dollar, but the total reserves of the Treasury and the Fed together are only one-sixteenth of an average day's trading. So when the Fed and the Treasury intervene, it strikes me two things occur. One is that the assumption is that the government knows best, not on what is best for the economy although that is the premise, but in what direction the markets are going to go and therefore you end up with a speculative situation.

The second thing that occurs is when it speaks in terms of foreign coordination which is always a very responsible and sensible thing because it is better to act in concert in some ways than not, that, by definition, implicit quid pro quos develop; that is, if we ask the Japanese or the British or the French or Germans to intervene on behalf of what we want the direction of dollar to go, does that make the Federal Reserve Board and the Treasury then obligated at another point in time to intervene at the request of those governments?

The history of the last few years has been that private sector actors have not only been larger but they have been wiser than governments and almost psychologically have wanted to bet against governments.

And so my question to you is, as a general proposition, how long can we sustain the notion that governments can correctly intervene and with regard to this intervention, because as a general proposition but on any day-to-day basis there could be differentiations, it appears the dollar has weakened versus—again, despite intervention.

Have we lost any monies that you want to report to the Congress and the American people and have other foreign governments lost any money and is that an awkward signal?

Mr. GREENSPAN. Congressman, we have obviously debated this at great length within the Federal Reserve, with the Treasury, and the general conclusion is that in the broadest sense, the fundamentals will determine where the exchange rate will go over time. Nonetheless, there have been instances where in retrospect, and even at the time, it appeared as though there was some temporary imbalance in the markets which we have effectively countered, preventing the market, for example, cumulating downward or cumulating upward.

If you can catch the markets at the appropriate time, I think you can break the pattern that exists. I don't think you can do it often. I think you can do it at important points in time and we, with the Treasury, discuss those issues at quite considerable length before we do it, and we always do it jointly—or I should say that we come together and make judgments as to how we should do it, and with very rare exceptions it is a 50–50 Treasury-Federal Reserve deal.

In my experience, which has been 7 years at the Federal Reserve, we have never lost any money. Indeed, our capital gains have been rather substantially positive. But I wouldn't argue that that is the purpose, that one is doing exchange rate intervention for the purpose of obtaining capital gains, but we are very much acutely aware that we are dealing ultimately with taxpayer money and we have to be certain that we protect the taxpayer from any losses.

When I say that as far as my 7 years at the Fed are concerned, and I assume it goes back probably a longer period than that, there have been no material losses, that is partly the result of a general awareness on the part of monetary authorities. I don't also recall that there are these obligations to other governments although it is true that we are often approached by some of our central bank colleagues or finance ministers and there is a lot of ongoing discussion.

But it is basically that each action, to the extent that we do coordinate it, is taken on its own and on its own merits. We try to be cooperative, in the sense that when we see there are a destabilizing set of forces which may be only marginally related to the dollar, we would obviously consider whether it is in our interest to be of help in that regard, but those are very rare instances.

Mr. LEACH. With regard to this intervention, there have been no losses?

Mr. GREENSPAN. That is correct.

Mr. LEACH. Good. Thank you.

Chairman KANJORSKI. Mr. Orton.

Mr. ORTON. Thank you, Mr. Chairman, and Dr. Greenspan a pleasure to see you again.

A few weeks ago as you appeared before the Budget Committee on which I sit, we had a brief interchange about the international exchange rate of the dollar, at which point you indicated you didn't have a lot that you could say.

I appreciate the comments you made today. I apologize I had to step out of the room a few minutes to deal with an issue back in my home district, so I didn't hear other responses you may have had, but there seems to be some confusion, at least on the part of many people I represent, about the dollar and the exchange rate of the dollar. And when the dollar is high, the reports from government are usually that the dollar is very strong, that it is very bad for foreign trade we get flooded with imports. Our exports are too costly, that slows down our economy. Therefore, we need to do something to intervene to lower the value of the dollar.

81-438 - 94 - 2

On the other hand, when the dollar is low, we are told the argument that you have made that this is now injuring our economy. We cannot have a dollar that is low and people are confused by saying, well, you know, what is a high dollar and what is a low dollar and when it is high, why does it have to be lowered and when it is low why does it have to be highered. And who is out there pushing this thing up and down and so forth? And there is a growing skepticism among the population that if we do know what we are doing, we are keeping it hidden from the public and that in fact someone is out there manipulating the dollar up and down and so forth.

When you see the new derivatives actions in the markets and you see a great deal of activity taking place there, this even fuels the skepticism and the speculation that there those bankers go again. You know, they are just controlling this policy and feathering their own nests and on and on and on.

It is my concern, I think, that we in government need to understand monetary policy. I think that we need to show the confidence to the public that we do know what is going on and why it is going on and that in fact either there is an open and free market or if it is a controlled market that it is controlled, but it is controlled by someone who knows what is going on and they are doing it for a good public purpose.

I am not asking you to disclose to us and the world what the basic secrets of monetary policy might be, if there are any such, but I guess I would like from you some indication about the extent of intervention, how often the Federal Reserve and the Treasury Department get together and intervene in the value of the dollar and the mechanism that is used for that intervention when it is required so that we can set to rest this skepticism that we are never satisfied or we don't have any policy or that we are running it up and down for some private gain or government gain.

Do you have any comments that you could help us?

Mr. GREENSPAN. Congressman, actually the first part of the question I was asked at the Kerrey Commission a week ago Friday in which the notion was raised of whether speculators can manipulate the dollar up and down. I would suspect that within very short periods of time—minutes, seconds—it is possible that somebody can unload a big loss and the amount purchased back or something like that. But these markets are extraordinarily efficient in the sense that they are free and open, and I know of really no incidences of where a significant private individual or a group of private individuals acting in concert were able to do very much with respect to moving any of the major currencies.

With respect to central bank and finance ministry intervention, the first step is for the senior staff in the Federal Reserve and the Treasury to consult with each other. Then I will talk with Under Secretary Summers or Secretary Bentsen and we will eventually come to a conclusion as to whether it is desirable to intervene or not. When a judgment to intervene is reached, the action is carried out by the fiscal agency of the Treasury which is the operating desk of the Federal Reserve Bank of New York.

This is a relatively rare action and is not a continuing issue. We either announce the action concurrently or eventually make a full report. We have not had in any memory that I can recall any major disputes. Sure, we have differences over the years but when it is apparent that some intervention should occur, it is usually a consensus view.

Mr. ORTON. Is there some level at which every time it is down you want it up and every time it is up we want it down? Is there some basic policy that identifies it is at the right place or are we really just relying on international markets and what happens with interest rates overseas and here and trade levels and so on?

Mr. GREENSPAN. I don't want to get into the details of that sort of thing.

All I can say is we endeavor to get a sense of what these markets are doing and from the American point of view recognize when we are dealing with these very large global international financial systems we have no alternative but to make certain that we are aware and if we find actions are helpful, initiate them. I don't think we would basically have a list of A, B, C, D. These are much too complex issues to have a simple laundry list of what you do, and if we did, I would be very uncomfortable.

Mr. ORTON. Thank you, Mr. Chairman.

Chairman KANJORSKI. Thank you very much, Mr. Orton.

The gentleman from Ohio, Mr. Fingerhut.

Mr. FINGERHUT. Thank you, Mr. Chairman. It is good to see you again, Chairman Greenspan.

Mr. GREENSPAN. Thank you.

Mr. FINGERHUT. I want to just stay for a moment longer on this issue of the dollar because I think it has given those of us who have been trying to watch the monetary and fiscal policy closely some concern. And fairly or unfairly, the reports of this same testimony that you gave before the Senate has focused on and the media reports of your testimony has focused on the impression that you indicated that the low dollar is a primary concern of yours with respect to inflation and that in itself might trigger the Fed to move again on the subject of interest rates, so it has become the focus of this round of testimony whether you intend it to be or not.

The question that I would ask you to explore a little further for us is two things. One, is it the value of the dollar itself that concerns you and concerns our central bank and that might lead you to act, or is it only to the extent that the value of the dollar, in fact, translates itself into inflationary pressures as a result of rising cost of imports, and so forth, so that if those inflationary pressures do not materialize, if, for example, the foreign companies, particularly Japanese companies who export their products to this country, eat some of the profits or eat some of the losses, as has been suggested, that some imports they might strategically use to maintain market share or for other reasons that you would then say, well, we watched with concern appropriately but we don't see this translating into actual impact and therefore we find it prudent not to act.

The second part of that as you answer is how much of this truly is a reflection of what is happening in the dynamic and changing economies of our trading partners and how much of it relates to our own economy which for better or for worse—some of us on this side think for better, some of our colleagues on the other side may think for worse—has been at a relatively stable fiscal monetary policy now for about 18 months to almost 2 years.

Mr. GREENSPAN. The focus that we have on the dollar is because it has an impact on the American economy. It has an impact one, for the reasons of the internal price effect which I mentioned in my prepared remarks, and also because of the crucial importance that with the very large amount of dollar-denominated assets in the world, what we don't wish to see happening is a loss in confidence in the productiveness of dollar-denominated assets. As a consequence of that, we are very much aware of how among a number of other things the dollar, the trend of the dollar affects the view as to what is happening in the United States.

The dollar often signals what the rest of the world's view is of the American economy which is quite relevant to us as a policy matter. I grant you that you have to be very careful when you have an exchange rate. There are two parties and it is quite conceivable that one party may have an impact on the economy of the other party that may be quite relevant to what is going on and that is one of the things we basically look at. We don't, as far as the overall focus of monetary policy is concerned, look to stabilizing the exchange rate merely to stabilize the exchange rate.

It is only to the extent that it has an important impact and implication on how the American economy is doing and it is one factor, a rather important one, of what determines on many occasions what our policy stance is. I can tell you, there are times when movements in the dollar are really of very marginal significance to policy. There are other times when they are quite important and important as to what they indicate about what may be going on among investors around the world in dollar-denominated assets.

So I can't give you a specific set of rules. As I said, we don't have a laundry list but the issues you raised are ones that we think about and we are concerned about in making appropriate judgments.

Mr. FINGERHUT. I appreciate the exchange will never get us the precision that we are seeking, but I guess I would just ask one followup to this point before moving on to another subject and ask whether you have any tentative conclusions that you would care to share with us as to whether this current round of instability and the exchange rates reflects fundamental long-term problems that you think need to be addressed by policy changes or whether it is simply one of those periods of time where there is instability because there is so much instability and uncertainty that surrounds the world economy?

Mr. GREENSPAN. Under Secretary Summers addressed this issue in the Senate yesterday and I found his evaluation a reasonable one, and indeed, prior to that statements by the Secretary of Treasury. And I would have very little to add to those statements.

Mr. FINGERHUT. Thank you.

Mr. Chairman, I know that my time is expired, if I could have one other question. It strikes me that one of the areas for which there is occasionally some speculation, and some are critical, you deserve a great deal of praise and this administration deserves a great deal of praise as it is appropriately seeking to coordinate monetary and fiscal policy.

I don't mean coordinate in advance, I mean coordinate in fact when the Congress and the administration together sought to begin to address the budget deficit which necessarily results in a contract of fiscal policies. The Federal Reserve, I think, appropriately accommodated that policy effort by maintaining its accommodative monetary policy until you no longer felt that was necessary. That was the gist of your testimony. You have also correctly identified, I think, the continued progress on the Federal budget deficit is a desirable policy goal, and I think that certainly the members I see up at this table wouldn't disagree with that.

But continued progress on the Federal budget deficit problem requires a continued, indeed, a racheted-up, further tightening of fiscal policy from this body and from the administration. The question is whether you would see the Federal Reserve to be in a position to continue to reflect its monetary policy, continue to balance its monetary policy, or accommodate its monetary policy to the fiscal policy if indeed the Congress is successful in making the steps on the Federal budget deficit that you indicated are desirable.

Mr. GREENSPAN. Congressman, last year when the Budget Program was put in place, I testified I believe before this subcommittee, and certainly before the Budget Committee, and it was my judgment that we would find that interest rates would fall as a consequence of budget actions because there was an inflation premium, as best as I could judge, embodied especially in long-term interest rates which reflected the concerns that markets had that after the turn of the century the deficit would begin to move up.

So we did not in conscious manner feel the necessity in addressing monetary policy to that particular fiscal policy stance because it wasn't, as we say in the textbooks, fiscal drag; that is, suppression of the economy, because from what we could judge, the decline in long-term interest rates, occurred as a consequence of budget policy, to a large extent and offset the so-called fiscal drag. In our judgment, that led us to conclude that no offsetting action was either appropriate or called for, and all I can say to you is that we consider what the Treasury is doing in this financing operation as a major element in the decision which we at the central bank are involved in with respect to policy and we have to coordinate because there is only one economic policy in the country.

You cannot have divergent policies and in the context which is very important to us and the Nation—the independence of the Federal Reserve as a central bank—we have endeavored to find the appropriate pattern of mix that in our judgment leads to a noninflationary economic growth. And in that regard, I must say we obviously talk quite often, I talk to Secretary Bentsen probably more than once a week in discussing this.

Mr. FINGERHUT. Would you judge—I promise, Mr. Chairman, I will absolutely stop after this followup. But would you judge that based on that answer to the actions last summer that further fiscal tightening on the part of the Congress to further efforts to reduce the deficit would result in the same impact on the markets at this stage or would it create a fiscal drag that would require some offset? Do you think that same inflation premium is there to be reduced?

Mr. GREENSPAN. I will say that long-term interest rates would be lower than they would otherwise be if we address the long-term post year-2000 deficit. Remember, when you are dealing with long-term bonds, it is the inflation expectation over the full maturity of the bonds and supply and demand reflects that. As a consequence, if the Congress makes a material change in the outyears, legislation that is enacted now but doesn't take effect until the outyears would have a positive effect on the financial markets.

Mr. FINGERHUT. I thank you, Mr. Chairman.

Thank you, Chairman Kanjorski, for your indulgence.

Chairman KANJORSKI. Thank you very much.

Now our friend from New Jersey, Mr. Klein.

Mr. KLEIN. Thank you, Mr. Chairman.

Chairman Greenspan, good morning. Good to see you again as always. I happen to subscribe to the view that a continuing robust growth in the economy is more important than the question of inflation, and I know that that may be somewhat at odds with your own view, but I do have some questions and I think most of them are in the framework of that time fix.

First of all, to follow up on the questions of Mr. Fingerhut and others who have asked about monetary policy, isn't the primary weakness of the dollar against the yen, and to a certain extent the German mark, rather than other countries' currency such as Canadian and other major trading partners?

Mr. GREENSPAN. Obviously, it differs in the sense that the dollar versus the yen in the market has come down quite considerably recently and obviously recovered the last week or so.

But it is certainly the case that the Canadian dollar is a very relevant currency to the United States because of the extraordinary amount of trade between us and the Canadians. There are a number of our Latin America trading partners whose exchange rates are important to us. We look at not only the individual currencies but also at what we call the trade-weighted data, depending on whether or not it is the major countries' exchange rates—the G–10—or whether it is even broader. They actually tell you different things.

You use them for different purposes for evaluation and obviously when you are dealing in the issues of psychology and inflation expectations and the like, the major currencies are far more important than a number of the other ones, but you can't disregard the others. They ultimately determine whether or not there are changes in import prices and therefore have an effect on domestic prices. So you can't disregard those other currencies.

Mr. KLEIN. Well, I realize you can't disregard them, but I am not sure you answered my question which specifically is—isn't the weakness against primarily the yen and the German mark?

Mr. GREENSPAN. As against the European countries, yes.

Mr. KLEIN. And if that be the case, should we be directing our policy primarily because of a weakness against those currencies?

Mr. GREENSPAN. I can't answer that very specifically, Congressman, because it depends on a lot of other issues that are involved in the markets and how the American economy generally is moving. But all I can say to you is that we are aware of the distinction and it does matter and it has different effects in different contexts and we try as best we can judge to get a sense of the overall exchange rate or more importantly the position of the dollar in international finance and how it affects domestic American economy.

Mr. KLEIN. Let me ask you one more question on currency and that is, is there any fear on the part of foreign investors that there may be further rises in American interest rates and does that have an effect on the strength of the dollar?

Mr. GREENSPAN. It is hard for me to judge what the psychology of markets is. Individual participants——

Mr. KLEIN. Let's assume for the moment that there is some fear on the part of foreign investors that that may occur. Would that have an effect on the strength of the dollar?

Mr. GREENSPAN. I have sort of diverted myself as best I can over the years from answering questions which are too hypothetical because the response would depend to a very large extent on what other events were occurring.

Mr. KLEIN. Let me just switch to another area and you talked earlier in response to one question about the fact that single-family home starts had declined. And while you didn't say so directly, isn't a major factor the fact that interest rates have gone up and to the extent that they have gone up, we are now experiencing a very sluggish experience in a major portion of the economy; namely, the home building industry?

Mr. GREENSPAN. You could certainly say that housing starts have come off their peaks; that is, housing sales are not as strong as they were in the latter part of 1993, for example. They are still quite solid and the crucial issue here is——

Mr. KLEIN. I don't think the home building industry will agree with you.

Mr. GREENSPAN. I do not deny that. The question really, basically, is if you want a viable home building industry, the thing that we in government can do most effectively to ensure it is to keep inflation expectations and inflation down.

Because under those conditions, you get far lower real interest rates, real mortgage rates, and you get a much more viable residential market. Just to respond in part to the question that you raised at the very beginning, Congressman, the question of growth versus inflation; implicitly it is my view, and I think the evidence is quite persuasive in this regard, is that a necessary condition to sustain long-term growth, whether it is residential building, automobiles, or anything else, is a low inflation rate.

Mr. KLEIN. Well, since I am told that my time has expired, I will not belabor the issue, but thank you very much, Mr. Chairman.

Mr. GREENSPAN. Thank you, Congressman.

Chairman KANJORSKI. Thank you very much, Mr. Klein.

Mr. Chairman, earlier in order to let the whole panel have a question, I want to get back to something that is important and you just mentioned in your testimony the importance in your estimation of the independence of the Fed to be the determiner of domestic policy, and as you may be aware, this subcommittee has been fairly supportive of that thought process, but there are forces in the Congress and the United States that do not necessarily agree with the maintenance of the independence of the Fed as it is presently structured. And that brings us to some of the fears that I have.

And we have not had an opportunity to go into it, but as you and I know, there has been a request for the Federal Reserve to exercise prerogatives to take a seat on the banking international summits and I have always wondered whether or not that would constitute some sort of question on challenging the authority of the President and the Constitution to carry on this mandate of being the sole determiner of foreign affairs in the United States and to carry out foreign policy or whether this would put the Federal Reserve at some point in time in some future Presidency potentially in conflict with the domestic independence that they exercise.

And I understand, the decision on this has been run through the highest level of the administration, I have read all of their letters, some of the studies were forwarded to me by the Federal Reserve, but in my own mind I am not yet satisfied that we are to maintain the domestic independence of the Federal Reserve and the present legislation and withhold the pressures within the Congress to examine that question, that it is a propitious time to exercise the taking of that seat unless we clearly define parameters in which that seat would be exercised and operated by your membership on that board.

And even though this administration has apparently no objection to that, I am not sure this administration is viewing the long-term constitutional ramifications to the Office of the President and his effective carrying on of foreign policy for the United States and is there a way that we can, as I asked you before, perhaps have the time to have the best scholars in the country both from the constitutional standpoint and from an economic and international economic standpoint, help us out with this question.

In the past this issue has been brought up on two separate occasions, we took time to have very thorough studies by independent determiners and in both instances the recommendation in the Congress was to hold off on the exercise of that right. I think now without the benefit of the study and without the support system, I could see the pressures building in the Congress to look at the potentials of restructuring the structure of the Federal Reserve and to interfere at some point in time with its independence in establishing domestic policy if it appears that there is a conflict in international monetary policy and domestic American policy.

What is your response?

Mr. GREENSPAN. Mr. Chairman, you are raising an issue which is something we have all been considerably focused on. I might just say that the reasons why we did not take up our seat earlier was not, in my judgment, basically because of legal discussions that went on in an earlier period, but it just struck us as not to be the relevant time, although I was not involved, largely because it was not clear that the relationships we have currently with the BIS and have had for a very long period of time would be particularly enhanced if we were involved in some of the management decisions as to where the institution was going.

So I would say, first, that we did not perceive that there was any real purpose in our getting involved at the management level which is what being a member of the Board of Directors essentially implies. That has changed, and the reason it has changed, and the major issue that confronts, us is that as globalization of markets moves apace, there are going to be a number of institutions which are going to have a very important place in international finance. The BIS, in my judgment, is going to be one of those major ones, and, in my judgment, it is important for the United States to participate with our other colleagues in the institution to make certain that where that institution is going at least coincides, as best we can make it, with the interests of our country.

If we maintain the current position, which is essentially appearing at meetings periodically, we will not get the full benefits that I perceive it is possible for the United States to have from being on the board and having material impact.

I certainly don't deny that the issues you are raising concern very profound constitutional questions and one of the reasons why the very first thing that we did was to approach the Secretary of the Treasury and the Secretary of State and get a judgment from them on the legal, constitutional questions as they saw them, as well as the other appropriate issues which are related to whether or not we would gain benefits from being there.

As I indicated to you in a letter, Mr. Chairman, we are, of course, already involved fairly heavily, that is the Federal Reserve, in a number of other international financial institutions. I serve, for example, as the Alternate Governor in the International Monetary Fund.

I and my colleagues spend a great deal of time in discussions with a number of these international institutions and are heavily involved with them. In all of that, however, we are acutely aware, and we endeavor to make certain, that it is the decisions of the President of the United States that ultimately prevail on issues of international financial policy as it does on foreign policy.

We, as a consequence, have every intention of keeping the Secretary of the Treasury and the Secretary of State fully informed as to what we are doing. And should they raise issues which we think are relevant, it is important for us to make certain that we basically consult with them to make certain that whatever concerns they may have are duly addressed.

Chairman KANJORSKI. Mr. Chairman, I appreciate the fact and we are talking perhaps in the future and I appreciate the fact that the United States should probably be represented on the bank board, but I guess my problem is that I don't understand. And that bank very easily may start to become a major international monetary policy bank.

Mr. GREENSPAN. I would doubt that.

Chairman KANJORSKI. But it has the possibility. We, individually, have no control over what it may eventually evolve into.

Mr. GREENSPAN. My judgment is that that is not what it is structured for nor is it likely to emerge in that regard.

Chairman KANJORSKI. What will happen, Mr. Chairman, is as you are exercising that seat as Chairman of the Federal Reserve, if it has some conflict or effect on the domestic policy of the United States, are you going to accept an order from the President of the United States to restrict or change monetary policy on a domestic level and interfere with the independence? That sets a precedence to interfere with the independence if that order is issued with the President carrying out the foreign policy of the United States.

Mr. GREENSPAN. First of all, it is an issue which I don't perceive ever arising—the issue of monetary policy and independence, which, of course, as you know, is that the decisions that we make are not subject to question by the executive branch. Over the years, and this goes back two or three generations, there has been an awareness in the Federal Reserve of this whole question of our international financial relationships.

I don't recall instances, although I suspect there may well be a few, in which the issue of an independent monetary policy by the central bank in this country has basically been undercut by the executive branch subsequent to the 1951 accord, in which, you may recall, there was an agreement between the Treasury Department and Federal Reserve to disengage from what really was mandated support for certain Treasury securities issues.

We are sensitive to the questions and the concerns that you raised and because we think that independence is such a crucial question, I cannot imagine that we as an institution would allow ourselves to be put in a position whereby the type of problem you are concerned about would arise.

Chairman KANJORSKI. Rather than finding the support of discussion on the issue of some of the pending legislation that would restrict the nature and makeup of the Federal Reserve independent banking institution, would you have any hesitancy in holding off a final decision and in assuming that seat until this subcommittee is able to have a roundtable hearing, perhaps even in camera, so that we could have ultimate determination of what the scholars in constitutional law feel the ramifications of such a decision may be?

Mr. GREENSPAN. Mr. Chairman, I think that would create a problem for us because the process is very far advanced and the reason we went to the State Department and indeed to the Foreign Relations Committees of both Houses very early on was to get precisely this constitutional question addressed. I can conceive that there will be those, as in all constitutional questions, who would find a reason to suggest that this is inappropriate.

It is a very complex issue and it probably, Mr. Chairman, really gets too far beyond the questions of the BIS. It really raises issues of what our relationship is with the IMF and the World Bank and a whole variety of other things.

Chairman KANJORSKI. Some of the pending legislation, Mr. Chairman, would get into those issues and I am trying to avoid——

Mr. GREENSPAN. All I can say to you, Mr. Chairman, is that it is so crucial that we, as the most important central bank in the world by size, in a very, very detailed manner integrate our views and our actions with the international financial system because that, in my judgment, very strongly serves the interests of this country. Were we going to an isolationist mode, which would pull us away from the extraordinary role that we have played since the end of World War II, would be to America's disadvantage. If you took this question very broadly about the constitutional issue, I am not sure where it stops. I do think it probably means that the central bank would have great difficulty dealing in the international financial sphere, and in my judgment that would probably be most detrimental to our system.

Chairman KANJORSKI. I just think that the Representatives of the United States of America should be responsive internationally to the President of the United States and to his command in carrying out foreign policy, and I think if we interpose the independent central bank of the United States in that role without fully examining what we are doing and understanding it, I think that delicate balance could be set off and it could cause a great deal more pressure on the domestic policy to rein in the independence of the Federal Reserve.

Mr. GREENSPAN. I must say I certainly hope not because if you ask me academically whether or not I see some very major questions that relate to central bank involvement in these various different types of institutions, I would have to agree with you. In fact, there is a question that comes up. I hope those issues have been resolved as a practical matter because there are innumerable things that institutions in this government with respect to which the Constitution is too broad to specify what they should or should not do, and we have considerable difficulty with that.

We have given a great deal of thought to this question. As I indicated earlier, it is one of the reasons why we approached the legal advisor at the State Department very early on, to raise precisely the questions that you are raising.

Chairman KANJORSKI. And I took that into consideration, but I have also talked with a number of experts and officials who are tangentially involved in the issue and they think that perhaps there may be a very strong future constitutional question.

Mr. GREENSPAN. Let me say if there is an issue, Mr. Chairman, it is such a broad issue that it goes way beyond the Bank for International Settlements, and it is a fundamental issue with respect to an independent central bank in our society.

Chairman KANJORSKI. I agree with you, Mr. Chairman, but as you know there is a great deal of legislation pending in the Congress to get into this whole thing. At this point, to defend the independence of the Federal Reserve, we have not gone that distance but now this just may be the straw that requires that movement. I would hope that we carry on some continued dialog on that.

Mr. GREENSPAN. By all means. This much broader question is quite an important issue which I think all institutions in the American Government should be subject to.

Chairman KANJORSKI. My good friend from Utah, Mr. Orton.

Mr. ORTON. Thank you, Mr. Chairman. I do have one other brief question which I will make sure that—I may have asked you previously; if so, I apologize and you can just tell me so.

But as most of us agree, the trade policy of this Nation and tax policy do have an impact on monetary policy and vice versa as well as economic growth. As we have examined tax policy around the world, and see the United States being the only one of our major trading partners that does not have a border adjustable type of tax, like a value-added tax which is added on imports as they come into the country and taken off exports as they go out, many have suggested that this is giving us an economic disadvantage in our own and world trade markets and many, including the current chairman of Ways and Means, Mr. Gibbons, have recommended that we adopt such a type of tax which could be border adjustable.

My question to you would be if the United States were to adopt such a tax, do you believe that it would have any impact on monetary policy, positive, negative, or just tangential impact on economic growth and trade?

Is there any issue of monetary policy, anything that we in this subcommittee should be concerned about or need to hear from you with regard to that type of a tax system, assuming that it were not just added to our current taxes so you are not taking more tax revenue out of the economy?

Mr. GREENSPAN. It is a shift.

Mr. ORTON. If it were to replace a current type of tax so that the same level of taxes were taken out of the economy but done so in a different manner.

Mr. GREENSPAN. Congressman, I think that a value-added tax, especially as a substitute for other taxes, has very profound implications with respect to savings and investment in the United States and to the extent that that impacts on our underlying economy, the central bank has to address that. It is hard for me to tell you in advance precisely how it would impact but there is nothing in the procedure that you are discussing which in any way creates a problem for us and there is no reason why we will not be able to adjust accordingly if it is required. So how you pursue the discussions with respect to this question shouldn't need to be concerned with whether we would be able to appropriately adjust. I see no reason why we should not be.

Mr. ORTON [presiding]. OK. Thank you. Since the chairman is currently tied up, I will turn to Mr. Neal.

Mr. NEAL. Thank you, sir. Mr. Chairman.

I would like to thank you again for your continuing good job keeping an eye on inflation and keeping it as low as possible. I go out of my way to say that every time I can because I think usually you get criticism when you have to raise short-term rates to try to look out for the longer term well-being of our economy. And I just want you to know that I appreciate it and think that most people do appreciate it. Most people do understand that the fight against inflation is clearly the most important endeavor that you can engage in and you all have done a good job with it in recent years.

Mr. GREENSPAN. Let me just say thank you.

Mr. NEAL. Well, thank you.

In that regard, I read some conflicting stories about your comments the other day concerning the use of monetary policy for purposes of possibly changing the dollar-yen relationship in particular but essentially changing the value of the dollar.

As I understand it, the real problem is not a dollar problem, but it is a yen problem. The dollar has maintained its fairly consistent relationship with most of the currencies of the world. I understand there has been a little change relative due to the German currency, but other than that, the major change has taken place in the relationship between the dollar and the yen, and it seems to me that that is primarily a yen problem. The Japanese are running a large surplus with the rest of the world, and this is sort of the way the world adjusts to that situation, by changing the value of their currency which will ultimately change the value of their trade relationship.

And isn't it true that just as we wouldn't want to use monetary policy to temporarily boost employment because we know that the costs would be great to employment later on, we wouldn't want to use monetary policy to manipulate the value of the currency? Is that correct or not? I am really trying to understand that.

Mr. GREENSPAN. I would say, Congressman, as I have testified before this subcommittee on several occasions, that the value of the dollar is one of the elements which we think are important in making judgments of what our domestic monetary policy should be. It is very difficult to imagine a case where it would be the sole consideration. That would be an extreme which I find utterly unlikely, but nonetheless it is a factor which we consider, and there are a number of other factors which are involved in policy. We try to balance them and try to make judgments because we have only one monetary policy. We only have a single activity which we can implement that largely in today's current context is the Federal funds rate—in an earlier context it was the net borrowed reserves. But the point of issue is that at any particular time there is only one policy and there are innumerable things which are involved in making a judgment as to how we calibrate that and the exchange rate is clearly one of them.

I don't want to comment on the specifics of individual currencies, but we endeavor to make judgments as to, when currencies move, whether it is the dollar that is relevant or whether it is the other currency. Obviously, it is a bilateral relationship and there are occasions when it is one and there are occasions when it is the other and there are occasions when it is both.

Mr. NEAL. Let me ask a related question. I notice that you have a brief discussion in your remarks of leading economic indicators that you use to try to set the proper monetary policy or properly control inflation. It often occurred to me—and again I am not a technician in this area but an interested observer—that long-term interest rates might be the very best indication of future inflation because they reflect not only the current monetary policy but essentially a huge pool involving all the investors of the world which then reflects inflationary expectations.

Now, as I understand it, the reason you couldn't use that as a sole tool—I don't know if you want to or not—I would be interested to know. I wish you would comment on that. It would be one of the best indicators, but even if you did, you probably couldn't use it as the sole tool because it would be hard to separate out real inflation from inflationary expectations. And in that regard, I know that you have commented before that you thought it might be a good idea for us to be able to issue inflation indexed bonds which would give us a more clear measure of that.

You know, Congressman Doug Barnard had introduced a bill to encourage the issuance of inflation indexed bonds and I have introduced that bill again. Would you like to comment on that and tell us if you think the passage of that would be useful to you and how?

Mr. GREENSPAN. Unquestionably, Congressman. The advantages of having indexed bonds, especially if we have them across a spectrum of maturities, is it would give us and other members of the economic policy fraternity in this government a reasonably good sense of judgment as to what the inflationary expectations are at various different maturity levels.

I think you are correct in distinguishing between actual inflation and inflationary expectations. Inflationary expectations sometimes are a good indicator of what actually materializes; sometimes they are not.

Nonetheless, the very expectations themselves are a very crucial variable in the way the economy functions. That is, even if inflation expectations are wrong, their impact on the structure of the way the economy goes is impervious. As to whether or not they are right or wrong, the effect is there, and as a consequence we have to focus on those variables to know what it is the markets are effectively assuming.

The basic question for the Treasury Department in considering this is whether or not this can be done without any cost to the taxpayer, and there are those who argue that pension funds would be very big buyers of these types of instruments. You might have a larger market for your securities by disaggregating them into certain pieces where certain individual purchasers would find a use for these indexed bonds.

There is another question as to whether in fact the volumes can be large enough so that the bid-asked spread is the same as it is in all of the nonindexed bonds, because if you have a larger spread, even one basis point, it does have an effect on the economy, it does have an effect on the cost to the taxpayers. So these are a lot of judgments that have to be made, but from the point of view of economic policymaking and international monetary policymaking, there is no question that such indexed bonds would make an important contribution to the policy deliberative process.

Mr. NEAL. Sounds like we should have some hearings on this and look into the costs and benefits.

Mr. GREENSPAN. I think that would be useful.

Mr. NEAL. Thank you.

Chairman KANJORSKI. The gentleman from Ohio, Mr. Fingerhut.

Mr. FINGERHUT. Thank you, Chairman Greenspan. You have been very accommodating. I will be very brief, but Mr. Neal actually brought us to the only question that I had restrained myself from in my first round and that was this very question of inflation expectation versus inflation.

Mr. Klein previously stated, I think, what is a common view in the public of a sense of frustration that just as the economy starts to seemingly respond at a more rapid pace providing better opportunities for our people, all of a sudden we feel like we are restraining it. And I join Mr. Neal in applauding your diligence and believing that the fight against inflation is critically important for long-term prosperity, and I hope my comments to you are reflective of that, but it is frustrating and indeed difficult to explain why we must fight not only inflation, that I can explain to people, but why we must fight expectations on the part of investors who are often moved by real factors in the marketplace but are occasionally moved by rumors and other factors.

I noted yesterday the dollar moved on the rumor the troops had crossed the line between North and South Korea and after that was not confirmed, that people backed off. I remember being on the floor of the House one day knowing that the stock market was moving on rumors of assassination attempts which, of course, proved to be untrue.

Is there not a role for the Federal Reserve to play in addressing those expectations on the basis of your actual knowledge of whether those expectations are accurate or not?

In reading your testimony, both the portions you delivered and the portions you didn't, you clearly—in the entire Federal Reserve System clearly there is no stone unturned in trying to find out whether or not inflation is a problem in our economy, the beige book, all of the comparisons and detailed analyses of various industries.

If you find that the exceptions don't correlate to your detailed investigation, is there not a role to play in saying that we believe those expectations are wrong so that perhaps we can turn down that premium without having to address it with higher interest rates?

Mr. GREENSPAN. Let me just say that while I would argue that inflation expectations are not a perfect forecaster of inflation, they are really quite good; that is, they do pick up a reasonable proportion of the variance that we have in such situations with actual inflation so that it is not as though it is a wholly random and meaningless set of numbers. It is largely the consequence of a very fair confluence of sophisticated views in the marketplace as to what is going on.

Some of the views are a little bit flaky. Some of them are really sort of dubious and even manipulative, maybe, but overall the system works remarkably well. It is a really impressive sight to see how this very complex financial system which we have in the United States functions and in my judgment creates a significant amount of real wealth for the average American. It is not just an abstraction.

The problem that we would have if we were to comment on rumors—and I grant you some of the rumors we know are true or false, indeed a lot of the rumors are about what we are doing—is that if you comment on some but not on all, you run into the problem: The Fed is not denying X, therefore it is confirmation. Or if one looks at the particular selection of the types of rumors that we try to get straight, it won't take the markets very long to figure out which ones we are avoiding and that will just merely cumulate the problem. So I can't see any real solution to this.

I am going to agree with you that there are a lot of judgments and actions that go on in the marketplace which are noises instead of decisions and there is no systematic basic reason for them. But I would say when you cut through all of that, it works pretty well, and it is working increasingly well as the years go on and the techniques improve and communications and telecommunication complexes emerge on the scene.

We have a far more efficient financial system than we did 10 years ago, 20, 30 years ago. And it is very complex and it lends itself, as indeed any complex system does, to problems at the margin.

I don't deny that there are problems, and, indeed, one of the reasons why we sometimes choose to intervene in the international financial markets is our judgment that some of the decisions that are being made by people are inappropriate to the real world and are having an effect which we think we can alter not by commenting but by action. And indeed that is one of the ways in which I would explain why it is we intervene.

Mr. FINGERHUT. Thank you. That is helpful. I think that my point is not that I would desire you to monitor the rumor mills in the markets and respond but rather to—and I think you do this quite frequently, but occasionally these testimonies give us a chance to say it again—to make clear that the Federal Reserve responds to those policies that they believe to be actually in fact occurring. Even if you believe the expectations are reasonable expectations, that is obviously a policy that needs to be responded or expectation that needs to be responded to as opposed to simply the perception that investors may—that we would be trying to confirm investors' expectations even if they have made a false judgment, and I think that is an important statement for the American people to have confidence to know that we are responding to actual policy.

Thank you, Mr. Chairman.

Chairman KANJORSKI. Thank you very much, Mr. Fingerhut.

Mr. Chairman, I just have one little question for you. I know that you are working very closely with the Secretary of Treasury on the introducing of the new $100 bills or currency to prevent counterfeiting, and I am just wondering whether or not we are going to have some sort of forced redemption period where that money would be introduced and to disqualify anyone keeping a horde of money beyond a certain period of time, maybe with an exception for widows finding $10,000 under the mattress, but other than that if we had a short redemption period of necessity for disclosure and cashing in for those funds, would that not serve as a major blow to organized and drug cartels and terrorist groups that are stashing away a large amount of cash?

Mr. GREENSPAN. Mr. Chairman, I wouldn't suspect that wouldn't have an effect on law enforcement. We have never in this country disavowed any of the Federal Government's obligations. Indeed, it is a fascinating thing to take a look at the statement of public debt. Still outstanding are a lot of 50 cent pieces from the Civil War which obviously are destroyed, a lot of gold certificates which are destroyed, but they are still an official obligation of the United States. The reason that choice was made is that there is a sense in which the American people have a certain relationship to their currency which I find extraordinary in the sense that if you try to change it, if you alter it in a way which makes them feel uncomfortable, the response is really quite surprising.

There is something very important about a government claim, and in my judgment, despite the fact that I don't deny that there are fairly significant crime prevention advantages in trying to do a number of these things, I think it is far more important that we continue this policy, which goes back to the beginning of our Nation, of honoring all of our liabilities.

Alexander Hamilton made some very important choices very early on in our country and that has essentially driven the Treasury Department ever since. To my knowledge there is no interest at this stage in trying to have a moratorium or I should say limit the legal tender nature of some of the claims that are existing.

It is an interesting issue and you may want to talk to the Secretary of the Treasury on that, but it is one that we have periodically come to grips with, and I personally am fascinated with how important the integrity of the currency is to American people.

Chairman KANJORSKI. I appreciate that, but I just thought this was a great way to get the green market in this country, certainly for the stashes of criminal activity as well, and at least giving the Congress the opportunity of discussing with the Fed and Treasury as to whether there should be a disclosure form with the capacity of tracing where these large portions of money come from for further prosecution.

I am struck with the romance that we have with the currency but presently pending on the floor, the FBI is attempting to have us allow for telephonic communications to be tapped so the privacy sometimes of Americans aren't necessarily thought of being as protected by this government as our currency is. That is interesting.

Mr. GREENSPAN. As best we can judge, more than half of our currency is abroad. That is an extraordinary phenomenon.

Chairman KANJORSKI. Mr. Chairman, we in our earlier discussion I sort of guaranteed I would try to get you out by noon. We have other questions from Mr. Ridge, our ranking member of the subcommittee and others. I would ask unanimous consent that they have 2 weeks to submit in writing questions and if you would be courteous enough to respond to that, we would appreciate it.

Are there other members of the subcommittee that would have questions?

Mr. NEAL. Do you have time for another question, Mr. Greenspan?

Mr. GREENSPAN. I will speak fast.

Mr. NEAL. If you do, let me ask you again on this question of leading indicators. It just seems to me that the comments that people make about monetary policy that are critical lately have fallen into two broad categories. One is that they say you are acting prematurely, that they can't see any inflation on the horizon and they don't see how you can, and therefore it is totally unjustified to raise short rates. And the other one has to do with this relationship between employment and inflation. People often say they think that we would—that you are threatening employment when you fight inflation.

Now, I think the evidence is pretty clear on the second point, both in our country down throughout history and other countries down throughout history, that employment is enhanced when we keep inflation under control and that means sometimes taking some unpopular actions to keep it under control, but the way to enhance employment is to keep inflation low and I think every opportunity I have to make that point I try to make it and you ought to make it.

And it is fascinating just as an aside on this, a very fascinating experience that occurred in another country, most fascinating because it appeared under a labor government and we often think of labor governments being for inflation. I am thinking here of New

Zealand where over the last several years New Zealand's economy was out of control. Huge deficits, runaway inflation, high unemployment, and so on. A labor government took the tough steps that were necessary to get their economy back under control. Now they have inflation under 2 percent, they have economic growth 6 or 7 percent, employment is rising, they still have some unemployment. But they are moving in the right direction.

And then this other point on leading indicators, if you—I just think if you said more about it, that it would help. It would just help maintain support for the anti-inflation policy. I wonder if you would just take a minute to comment on that. Aren't long-term interest rates one of the better leading indicators of future inflation?

Mr. GREENSPAN. To the extent, Congressman, that we can infer the inflation expectation part of those long-term rate changes, then I think it is very helpful and one of the things that we try to do is differentiate between the real rate of increase in long-term bonds and that component which represents changes in inflation expectations.

Mr. NEAL. I understand that is difficult. I think that was what Mr. Fingerhut was trying to get at here. If you could separate those out and then, of course, the way you said that, we can separate that out is to issue inflation index bonds, which we can talk about in more detail later and we will have a hearing on that. But that is a good indicator.

Mr. GREENSPAN. Yes, sir.

Mr. NEAL. Do you have any hesitancy? Let me try to get at this in another way. Is there some hesitancy about a full discussion about what you use as leading indicators? Is there——

Mr. GREENSPAN. No, the only hesitancy is that it varies from time to time and there is a whole array of things that we look at, depending on what we judge to be the important forces which are driving the economy at any particular point in time. And while we have an elaborate set of econometric models, they are actually too simplistic no matter how complex they are because they basically are fitted to a extended past period of time to get relationships, and it is very questionable about whether the economy's structure stays the same during that period.

There is no alternative to having a conceptual model of what we think is driving the economy. And that would include all the indicators with respect to inflation expectation as well as a variety of other elements. For example, back in the late 1980's, early 1990's, when we were dealing with the credit crunch, it became very clear to us that balance sheet strain was a very important element in how the overall economy was going to behave. That is a very rare event. Much of the time balance sheet strain doesn't exist, but for a period of time it was the most effective element in a model which guided us where we ought to be and we keep changing those roads and there is really no alternative to making a forecast and trying to understand the relationships as best we can.

And we have numbers of indicators. Some of them work well, some of them work not so well. I don't know if it was Mr. Fingerhut who raised the question of whether or not central banking is a science. The answer is it is not.

Mr. NEAL. So what you are saying is there are new elements that impact on the economy that are impacting in a stronger way than they have earlier. Today that might be the falling value of the yen, for example, something that wasn't a problem several years ago.

Mr. GREENSPAN. I have been reluctant to be very detailed about specific frameworks that we use because it creates problems for us in implementing policy. But if we sense that there are forces which are moving the economy one way or another, we try to understand them as best we can. And one thing we know is that the presumption that somehow we can implement monetary policy without making judgments about the future is false.

Mr. NEAL. Thank you.

Chairman KANJORSKI. Does the gentleman from North Carolina have any further questions?

Mr. NEAL. Well, not that I can't postpone.

Chairman KANJORSKI. I am going to prevail, if I can, on the more junior members of the subcommittee. We made Mr. Greenspan a promise and we haven't kept it by just a few minutes, but we thank you very much for your indulgence, Mr. Chairman. We look forward to our next meeting and we hope we can carry on the dialog we had a little earlier to see if we can we resolve some of those questions.

Thank you.

Mr. GREENSPAN. Thank you very much, Mr. Chairman.

[Whereupon, at 12:07 p.m., the hearing was adjourned.]

A P P E N D I X

July 22, 1994

Testimony by

Alan Greenspan

Chairman

Board of Governors of the Federal Reserve System

before the

Subcommittee on Economic Growth and Credit Formation

of the

Committee on Banking, Finance and Urban Affairs

U.S. House of Representatives

July 22, 1994

Mr. Chairman and members of the Subcommittee, I appreciate this opportunity to discuss with you recent economic developments and the Federal Reserve's conduct of monetary policy.

The favorable performance of the economy continued in the first half of 1994. Economic growth was strong, unemployment fell appreciably, and inflation remained subdued. To sustain the expansion, the Federal Reserve adjusted monetary policy over recent months so as to contain potential inflation pressures.

Our actions this year can be understood by reference to policy over the previous several years. Through that period, the Federal Reserve moved toward and then maintained for a considerable time a purposefully accommodative stance of policy. During 1993, that stance was associated with low levels of real short-term interest rates--around zero. We judged that low interest rates would be necessary for a time to overcome the effects of a number of factors that were restraining the economic expansion, including heavy debt burdens of households and businesses and tighter credit policies of many lenders. By early this year, however, it became clear that many of these impediments had diminished and that the economy had consequently gained considerable momentum. In these circumstances, it was no longer appropriate to maintain an accommodative policy. Indeed, history strongly suggests that maintenance of real short-term rates at levels prevailing last year ultimately would have fueled inflationary pressures.

Accordingly, the Federal Open Market Committee at its meeting in early February decided to move away from its accommodative posture by tightening reserve market conditions. Given the level of real short-term rates and the evident momentum in the economy, it seemed likely that a substantial cumulative adjustment of policy would be needed. However, Committee members recognized that financial markets were not fully prepared for this action. About five years had passed since the previous episode of monetary firming, and a number of market participants in designing their investment strategies seemed to give little weight to the possibility that interest rates would rise; instead, many apparently extrapolated the then-recent, but highly unusual, extended period of low short-term interest rates, fairly steady capital gains on long-term investments, and relatively stable conditions in financial markets. Many Committee members were concerned that a marked shift in the stance of policy, while necessary, could precipitate an exaggerated reaction in financial markets.

With this in mind, we initially tightened reserve conditions only slightly--just enough to raise the federal funds rate 1/4 percentage point. And the financial markets did indeed react sharply, with substantial increases in longer-term interest rates and declines in stock prices. Markets remained unsettled for several months, and we continued to move cautiously in March and April in the process of moving away from our accommodative stance. By mid-May, however, a considerable portion of the adjustment in portfolios to the new rate environment appeared to have taken place. With financial markets evidently better prepared to absorb a larger move, the Federal Reserve could substantially complete the removal of the degree of monetary accommodation that prevailed throughout 1993. The Board raised the discount rate 1/2 percentage point, a move that was fully passed through to reserve market conditions by the FOMC. Overall, the federal funds rate increased 1-1/4 percentage points during the first half of the year, and real short-term rates likely rose a similar amount. Partly to minimize any market confusion about the extent of and rationale for our moves, the Federal Reserve has announced each action and, in relevant instances, provided an explanation. At its meeting in early July, the FOMC faced considerable uncertainty about the pace of expansion and pressures on prices going forward, and it made no further adjustment in its policy stance.

Nonetheless, it is an open question whether our actions to date have been sufficient to head off inflationary pressures and thus maintain favorable trends in the economy. Labor demand has been quite strong, pointing to robust growth in production and incomes. To be sure, some hints of moderation in the growth of domestic final demand have appeared, and the recent indications of accelerating inventory accumulation may suggest an unwanted backing up of stocks. Conversely, the inventory accumulation may reflect pressures on firms who had brought inventories down to suboptimal levels and now need to replenish them. In the latter case, stock-building may continue at an above-normal rate, supporting production for quite some time. Moreover, the improving economic conditions of our trading partners should add impetus to aggregate demand from the external sector.

How these forces balance out in the coming months could be critical in determining whether inflation will remain in check, for the amount of slack in the economy, while difficult to judge, appears to have become relatively small. Concerns that productive capacity could come under pressure and prices accelerate are already evident in commodity and financial markets, including the foreign exchange market. An increase of inflation would come at considerable cost: We would lose hard-won ground in the fight against inflation expectations--ground that would be difficult to recapture later; our long-run economic performance would be impaired by the inefficiencies associated with higher inflation if it persisted; and harsher policy actions would eventually be necessary to reverse the upsurge in inflationary instabilities. We are determined to prevent such an outcome, and currently are monitoring economic and financial data carefully to assess whether additional adjustments are appropriate.

The economic figures that have formed the backdrop for our policy actions so far this year confirm that a rapid expansion has been in progress. Following growth at an annual rate of 7 percent in the fourth quarter of last year, real gross domestic product rose at nearly a 3-1/2 percent rate in the first quarter. A conceptually equivalent measure of aggregate output, gross domestic income, exhibited even larger gains in the fourth and first quarters. At this stage, available data leave some uncertainty regarding the pace of economic activity over the past three months. Nonetheless, the evidence in hand makes it reasonably clear that growth remained appreciably above its longer-run trend. The robust expansion over the first half of 1994 has been reflected in substantial increases in employment. Since last December, nonfarm payrolls have risen by 1-3/4 million workers, bringing the gain in jobs since the expansion got underway to 5 million. Reflecting this hiring, the civilian unemployment rate has fallen to 6 percent.

Although labor markets have tightened considerably in recent months, aggregate measures of wage and compensation rates have not yet evidenced persuasive signs of acceleration. Similarly, the increases in the consumer price index excluding food and energy, at about a 3 percent rate over the last six months, have remained near last year's pace, while the overall CPI has risen at a reduced rate of about 2-1/2 percent. To be sure, price pressures have been manifest at earlier stages of processing: Costs of many commodities and materials have been climbing, in some cases reflecting the tightening of industrial capacity utilization, which is now at its highest level in five years. But these pressures have been offset by favorable trends in unit labor costs resulting from marked improvements in productivity--especially in manufacturing--in recent years.

The accumulating evidence of stronger-than-expected economic growth here and abroad, combined with changing expectations of policy actions by the Federal Reserve as well as other central banks, prompted considerable increases in long-term interest rates in occasionally volatile markets over the first half of the year. Market participants concluded that, with aggregate demand stronger, higher real rates would be necessary to hold growth to a sustainable pace. Inflation expectations may also have been revised higher, as the performance of the economy seemed to make further near-term progress against inflation less likely and raised questions about whether price pressures might intensify.

To a degree, the very volatility of markets probably augmented the backup in long-term interest rates. One of the effects of the extended market rallies of recent years was to promote a rather complacent view among investors about the risks of holding long-term assets. In response, they gradually increased the proportions of their portfolios devoted to stocks and bonds, driving up their prices still further and narrowing risk spreads. But when developments earlier this year surprised investors and diminished their confidence in predicting future market conditions, they pulled back from long positions in securities until returns rose to compensate them for the additional price risk.

The recent weakness in bond prices was not limited to the United States, but was accompanied by a surge in foreign interest rates. This surge was particularly informative; ordinarily one would expect that as interest rates go up in one country, they would not increase to the same extent in others because exchange rates also would be expected to adjust. The initial jump in foreign interest rates was a sign of the extraordinary increase in uncertainty as, evidently, investors attempted to reduce their price-sensitive long positions by selling stocks and bonds regardless of currency denomination or economic conditions in the country of issuance. Roughly concurrently, moreover, signs that the slump in some foreign industrial economies was ending also were becoming apparent. As a result, market participants anticipated stronger credit demands abroad and a reduced likelihood of further easing by some foreign central banks, and intermediate- and longer-term rates in many of our trading partners rose as much as or more than in the United States.

Rising foreign interest rates, concerns in markets about the prospects for reduced trade tensions and about U.S. inflation contributed to considerable activity directed at rebalancing international investment portfolios. One effect of this activity appears to have been a substantial decline of the foreign exchange value of the dollar on net over the past six months. Foreign exchange rates are key prices in the American economy, with significant implications for the volumes of exports and imports as well as for the prices of imports and domestically produced items that compete with imports. The foreign exchange value of the dollar also can provide useful insights into inflation expectations. If we conduct an appropriate monetary policy--and appropriate economic policies more generally--we shall achieve our goals of solid economic growth and price stability, and such economic results will ensure that dollar-denominated assets remain attractive to global investors, which is essential to the dollar's continuing role as the world's principal reserve currency.

Rising interest rates and considerable volatility in financial markets do not seem to have slowed overall credit flows this year. At about a 5-1/4 percent annual rate through May, domestic nonfinancial sector debt has increased within its 4-to-8 percent monitoring range. The composition of debt growth, however, has differed from the patterns of the previous few years. Expansion of federal debt has slowed as the actions of the Congress and the Administration as well as cyclical forces have narrowed the budget deficit considerably. The total debt of businesses, households, and state and local governments, by contrast, has risen this year at a brisker pace, though growth has remained quite moderate in comparison with the average experience of recent decades. The pickup this year indicates both that private borrowers have become less cautious about taking on debt and that lenders have become more comfortable lending to them. Although household debt-income ratios remain high, debt-service burdens have fallen appreciably, partly reflecting the refinancing of mortgages at lower interest rates. The lower debt burdens evidently have fostered a more favorable attitude toward credit among households, and consumer installment borrowing has accelerated, with strong growth of consumer loans at banks. Banks have been increasingly willing to extend credit, easing their terms and standards on business loans considerably. In addition, some firms have turned to banks for financing because of the turbulence in bond and stock markets this spring. Total bank lending has strengthened materially and, with continued acquisitions of securities, total bank credit has picked up as well. Nonetheless, growth of the monetary aggregates remains damped, as banks have relied heavily on non-deposit sources of funds to finance loan growth.

Expansion of M2 has been quite slow this year, leaving this aggregate near the lower end of its 1-to-5 percent annual range. M3 actually has edged down, and thus is just below its 0-to-4 percent range for 1994. The weakness in the broader aggregates has not been reflected in the growth of income again this year, representing a continuation of the substantial increases in velocity that we have experienced over the past few years. The factors behind this behavior, however, have changed somewhat. The diversion of savings funds from deposits to bond and stock mutual funds, which sharply depressed money growth in past years, seems to have slowed substantially; the experience with capital losses this spring apparently has heightened some investors' appreciation of the risks of such instruments. On the other hand, rising short-term market interest rates, combined with the usual lag in the adjustment of deposit rates, have been a significant restraint on growth of the aggregates this year, in contrast to 1992 and 1993.

The increases in market rates this year have exerted a particular drag on the narrower monetary aggregates, as well as on the closely related reserves and monetary base measures. M1 has expanded at only a 4 percent rate so far this year, compared with 10-1/2 percent increases in each of the previous two years. M1's velocity has continued to fluctuate sharply, limiting its usefulness in formulating and interpreting monetary policy. The growth of M1 this year would have been even lower were it not for continued heavy demands for U.S. currency abroad. Flows of currency overseas have an even greater effect proportionately on the monetary base, which has growth rapidly this year despite declines in the reserves of depository institutions.

In reviewing its ranges for money growth in 1994, the FOMC noted that further increases in velocity of M2 and M3 were likely. Although yields on deposits will probably continue to rise further in lagged response to increases in market rates, the wider rate disadvantage of deposits is likely to persist, and savers will continue to redirect flows into market instruments. As a result, growth of both aggregates near the lower bounds of their 1994 ranges is considered to be consistent with achieving our objectives for economic performance, and the ranges were left unchanged.

The Committee also decided on a provisional basis to carry forward the current ranges for the monetary aggregates to 1995. We were not confident that we could predict with sufficient accuracy the money-income relationships that were likely to prevail next year to modify the ranges. Moreover, further permanent reductions of the monetary ranges did not seem necessary, as those ranges are already low enough to be consistent with the goal of price stability and maximum sustainable economic growth, assuming an eventual return to more stable velocity behavior. From that point of view, we felt that maintenance of the current monetary ranges would give the clearest indication of the long-run intentions of policy.

Regarding domestic nonfinancial sector debt, we made no adjustment to this year's monitoring range, but elected to set a provisional monitoring range for 1995 of 3 to 7 percent, a percentage point lower than this year's. A lower range would conform with some deceleration in nominal income, in the process of containing inflation and ultimately making progress toward price stability. The reduction is not intended to signal an increased emphasis on the debt measure, but it is supported by our view that rapid debt growth, if sustained, can eventually lead to significant imbalances that are inimical to stable, noninflationary growth. As usual, we shall review carefully all of the provisional ranges for 1995 in February.

Given the rapid pace of financial change, considerable uncertainties continue to attend the relationships of all of the aggregates to the performance of the economy and inflation, and we do not expect in the near term to increase the weight accorded in policy formulation to these measures. However, the processes of portfolio reallocation that have generated these recent shifts may be slowing. We shall continue to monitor monetary growth, and financial flows more generally, for information about the course of the economy and prices in coming to decisions regarding adjustments to the stance of monetary policy.

We expect that expansion of money and credit within the ranges we have established will be consistent with continuation of good economic performance. With appropriate monetary policies, the Board members and Reserve Bank Presidents see the economy settling into more moderate rates of growth over the next six quarters and inflation remaining relatively subdued. Specifically, the central tendencies of our forecasts are for real GDP to expand 3 to 3-1/4 percent over 1994 and 2-1/2 to 2-3/4 percent next year. The consumer price index is projected to increase 2-3/4 to 3 percent this year. In 1995, inflation may be about the same as in 1994 or slightly higher; the recent depreciation in the dollar is likely to put upward pressure on inflation over the next year if it is not reversed. With the pace of hiring likely to about match that of labor force growth, the unemployment rate is expected to remain close to its recent level.

In view of rapid economic growth recently and narrowing margins of slack in productive capacity, there has been considerable interest of late in the Federal Reserve's ideas about the long-run trends in output and employment consistent with avoiding pressures on prices. My colleagues and I don't think that numerical estimates of these trends by the FOMC would be useful in helping the Congress and the public gauge our policy strategy. We believe, instead, that our intentions are best conveyed in terms of our declared objective of fostering as much growth of output and employment as can be achieved without placing destabilizing inflationary pressures on productive resources. There is considerable uncertainty about what that goal implies for the expansion of GDP and rates of unemployment.

That said, it may be useful to note that the assumptions underlying the medium-term projections by the Administration and the Congressional Budget Office (CBO) are within the mainstream of thinking among academics and private business economists. These projections do not attempt to anticipate cyclical movements, but instead represent estimates of the likely performance of the economy in the neighborhood of its potential. The Administration, for example, projected in its most recent forecast that the economy will expand at a 2.5 percent rate in the second half of the 1990s and unemployment will average 6.1 percent. These projections are consistent with common estimates of the economy's potential growth rate and fall within the range of typical estimates of the so-called "natural rate" of unemployment.

Uncertainties around these estimates arise because identifying economic relationships is always difficult, partly owing to limitations of the data. But more fundamentally, all policymakers recognize that notions of potential GDP growth and the natural rate of unemployment are considerable simplifications, useful in conceptual models but subject to a variety of real-world complications. Our economy is a complex, dynamic system, comprising countless and diverse households, firms, services, products, and prices, interacting in a multitude of markets. Estimates of macroeconomic relationships, as best we can make them, are useful starting points for analysis--but they are just starting points.

Given questions about the aggregate relationships, policymakers need to look below the surface, in markets themselves, for evidence of tightness that might indicate whether inflationary pressures are indeed building. One important source of such evidence is the reports we receive from our Reserve Banks through their extensive contacts in their communities. These reports are released to the public in the "beige book" and are updated--frequently on the basis of confidential information from individual firms and financial institutions--by the Reserve Bank officials at our meetings and through normal intermeeting communications. Another source of useful information is individual industries and trade groups, which provide many timely indicators that are sensitive to supply-demand conditions in particular sectors.

If the economy were nearing capacity, we would expect to see certain patterns in the statistical and anecdotal information with increasing frequency and intensity. Reports of shortages of skilled labor, strikes, and instances of difficulties in finding workers in specific regions all would be more likely. To attract additional workers, employers would presumably step up their use of want-ads and might begin to use nonstandard techniques, such as signing or recruiting bonuses. More firms might choose to bring on less skilled workers and train them on the job. All of these steps in themselves could add to costs and suggest developing inflationary imbalances. As firms experienced difficulty in expanding production to meet rising demand, we would also expect to see increasingly frequent signs of shortages of goods as well as labor. Businesses might have difficulty in obtaining certain materials. Vendor performance would deteriorate, and lead times on deliveries of new orders would increase. Pressures on supplies of materials and commodities would be reflected in rising prices of these items.

Of course, we would not expect to see these phenomena occur simultaneously throughout the economy--quite the contrary. And, to a degree, these symptoms occur in a few sectors even in noninflationary economies. But a noticeable step-up in their incidence could constitute evidence of an incipient inflationary process.

In recent months, we have seen some of these signs. There are reports of shortages of some types of labor--construction workers and truck drivers, for instance. Indexes of vendor performance have deteriorated considerably, and manufacturers are paying higher prices for materials used in their production processes. As yet, these sorts of indications do not seem to be widespread across the economy. Nonetheless, we shall need to be particularly alert to these emerging signs in considering further adjustments to policy in the period ahead.

Financial flows may also impart useful warnings of price pressures. For example, persistent unsustainably low real interest rates might prompt very rapid credit growth, as expectations of price increases led households and firms to accelerate purchases of durable goods and equipment and finance these expenditures by stepping up the pace of borrowing. Although consumer borrowing has accelerated considerably of late, overall debt growth has so far remained moderate.

In light of the uncertainties about aggregate measures of our economic potential, the Federal Reserve cannot rely heavily on any one estimate of either the natural rate of unemployment or potential GDP growth. Most important, we have no intention of setting artificial limits on employment or growth. Indeed, the Federal Reserve would be pleased to see more rapid output growth and lower unemployment than projected by forecasters such as the CBO and the Administration--provided they were sustainable and consistent with approaching price stability. I should note, however, that most Federal Reserve policymakers would not regard the inflation projections of these other forecasters, which generally do not foresee further progress toward price stability over the medium term, as a desirable outcome.

A more significant issue for economic policymakers than the precise values of such estimates is what can be done to maximize sustainable employment and economic growth. We need, for example, to give careful attention to the problem of unemployment, as noted by the G-7 leaders at their recent summit. We could raise output and living standards around the world and at the same time ease many social problems if more people were working. Here at home, nearly eight million Americans are looking for work. At this stage of the business cycle--having experienced almost forty months of expansion and particularly strong growth recently--most of this unemployment probably is not due to a shortfall in aggregate demand. Rather, a good deal of it is likely "frictional," reflecting the ordinary process of workers moving between jobs, or "structural," resulting from longer-term mismatches between workers and available jobs. Monetary policy, which works mainly by influencing aggregate demand, is not suited to addressing such problems. But we ought to be encouraging other measures to increase the flexibility of our workforce and labor markets. Improving education and training and facilitating better and more rapid matching of workers with jobs are essential elements in making more effective use of the U.S. labor force. Just as important, Congress should avoid enacting policies that create impediments to the efficient movement of individuals across regions, industries, and occupations, or that unduly discourage the hiring of those seeking work. Competitive markets have shown a remarkable ability to create rising standards of living when left free to function.

Congress and the Administration also can continue to contribute to the growth of our economy's capital and productivity through a sound fiscal policy. The extension of the spending caps in last year's budget agreement was a significant step in putting fiscal policy on a more sustainable long-run path. Budget deficit reduction has proved to be particularly timely, by reducing the government's claim on savings just as households and firms are seeking more capital to finance investments. But under current law, the deficit as a percent of GDP will begin to expand again as we move into the next century, with unacceptable consequences for financial stability and economic growth. The primary cause of this increase will be federal outlays, which will almost surely again be rising at a pace that will exceed the growth of our tax base. Only by reducing the growth in spending is ultimate balance achievable.

As I have emphasized many times, the Federal Reserve also can contribute to the achievement of our overriding goal--maximum sustainable economic growth--by pursuing and ultimately achieving a stable price level. Without the uncertainties engendered by inflation, households and firms are better able to plan for the future. And firms focus on maximizing profitability by holding down costs and increasing productivity rather than by using inflationary conditions to support price increases. There is some evidence to suggest that the stronger trend of productivity growth we have witnessed over the recent past is due at least partly to the beneficial effects of low rates of inflation.

Our nation has made considerable progress in putting the economy on a sound footing in the past few years. To preserve and extend these advances, our monetary and fiscal policies will need to remain disciplined and focused on our long-term objectives; we would be foolish to squander our recent gains for near-term benefits that would prove ephemeral. Indeed, by fostering progress toward price stability, achieving lower federal budget deficits, and encouraging competitive markets both here and abroad, we will help ensure the continued vitality of our nation's economy now and for many years into the future.

U.S. House of Representatives

SUBCOMMITTEE ON ECONOMIC GROWTH AND CREDIT FORMATION
COMMITTEE ON BANKING, FINANCE AND URBAN AFFAIRS

109 FORD HOUSE OFFICE BUILDING
WASHINGTON, DC 20515-6054

TELEPHONE: (202) 226-7315

August 11, 1994

Hon. Alan Greenspan, Chairman
Federal Reserve System
20th Street & Constitution Avenue, NW
Room B-2125
Washington, D.C. 20551

Dear Mr. Chairman:

This letter is to thank you for your most recent participation in the *Conduct of Monetary Policy* hearing held by the House Banking Economic Growth Subcommittee on July 22, 1994. In addition, as I had mentioned at the close of the hearing, there are several questions which, in the interest of timeliness, I did not ask you directly at the hearing but intended to forward to you so that you could answer these in written form for the hearing record. As promised, I would like to submit the following five additional questions for your consideration.

- Recent concerns, regarding unprecedented stock market instability, the falling value of the dollar in the international currency markets, and the sustained high level of long-term rates, have raised different questions in regard to monetary intervention by the Federal Reserve. Particularly, in regard to the value of the dollar, in testimony you delivered on Friday, July 15, before the Bipartisan Commission on Entitlement and Tax Reform, you stated that the "U.S. economy has recently been experiencing the ideal combination of rising activity, falling unemployment, and slowing inflation." Yet in your testimony before the Senate on Wednesday, July 20, in addressing the falling value of the dollar, you stated that "the weak value of the dollar internationally is often indicative of possible domestic inflationary evidence" and is generally considered as bad for the economy. The value of the dollar in foreign markets has in fact fallen 5% since you testified before the Senate Banking Committee on May 27, and many have been expecting the Fed to raise rates as the most traditional way of defending a currency. You mentioned to the Subcommittee that you see the decline in the dollar as resulting from buying and selling trends for currency in foreign markets rather than from domestic inflation pressures. *At what point would you consider the falling value of the dollar to be severe enough in nature to warrant Fed intervention regardless of the perceived reasons for the dollar's decline, and do you see the value of the dollar as at all mitigating the positive statements you had about the state of the U.S. economy at the Bipartisan Commission hearing?*

- Although the nation continues to experience an economic recovery, there is evidence that this recent prosperity may not be widely dispersed. Despite strong GDP numbers and vigorous manufacturing productivity, wages have remained flat. For the roughly 6% of Americans who remain unemployed, job prospects for those at the low end of the skill level and wage spectrum are increasingly bleak. *Is there a role for monetary policy to play in alleviating this disparity, or as you suggested in your testimony before the Bipartisan Commission, in reaching this segment of the unemployed population, should we be concentrating on worker retraining and programmatic changes which connect dislocated workers with pockets of the job market in need of qualified workers? In addition, as these goals closely mirror the intent of H.R. 4040, the Reemployment Act of 1994, do you believe that the enactment of this legislation is desirable in order to alleviate the disparity which currently exists? Will enactment of*

Chairman Alan Greenspan
August 11, 1994
Page 2

retraining and reemployment legislation help to achieve the mandate of the `Humphrey-Hawkins´ Act to secure "the right of every American to full opportunity for useful employment at fair compensation?"

- Under the mandate of the Full Employment and Balanced Growth Act of 1978, a principle portion of your monetary policy report must contain a discussion of changes in the monetary aggregates and their relevance to the state of the economy. In the last ten to fifteen years, as you have often noted, the propensity for the aggregates, in particular M2, to meet their targets as outlined by the Fed has been infrequent. Many economists, including Dr. Geoffrey Moore at Columbia University, with whose work you are no doubt familiar, have attempted to include measures of non-monetary financial instruments in explaining the divergence of the monetary aggregates from their targets. *Has the Federal Reserve System continued to review such new modeling techniques and have they been useful in explaining why the aggregates have been declining in relevance for overall economic forecasting? If other non-monetary financial instruments are more meaningful indicators, what are they? Do you believe that the price of gold is a more reliable indicator for economic analyses?*

- The press release on the money supply issued by the Federal Reserve on July 21 showed that the growth rate in the monetary aggregate M2 for the three months ending in June, 1994 was zero. The smaller monetary aggregate, M1, has decelerated rapidly from its much higher growth rates last year to 1.6% in the last three months. Some experts, such as Dr. Anna Schwartz, predict that a continuation of this kind of slow or zero money growth could result in a recession. Would you please comment on the implications of this slow money growth.

- Many economists and analysts have been puzzled by the present levels for the price of gold which have not reached the psychologically "magic level" of $400 per ounce even though recent market tendencies such as flaccid bond values and a decrease in investor confidence would normally have caused an increase to this level. Over the past decade in particular, the international currency markets have become increasingly intertwined with activity in non-monetary markets, in particular that for gold. *Do you believe that it is within the mandate of the Federal Reserve System to participate financially in non-monetary markets to more effectively implement or enhance the affect monetary policy, and if so, under what circumstances?*

In addition, Congressman Tom Ridge, the Ranking Minority Member of the Economic Growth Subcommittee, who was unable to attend the hearing, asks that you respond for the record to the list of questions enclosed with this letter.

Thank you again for your consideration.

Sincerely,

Paul E. Kanjorski

Paul E. Kanjorski
Chairman, Subcommittee on Economic
Growth and Credit Formation

PEK/cpb

Questions for the Federal Reserve System Chairman from Congressman Tom Ridge, Ranking Minority Member of the House Banking Subcommittee on Economic Growth:

1. Mr. Chairman, have the monetary aggregates lost all significance to the point where we should transition to a gold-based system?

2. Is a return to the $350 gold price range desirable, and if so, why haven't the recent interest rate raises been successful in returning gold to this level?

3. How is it that this country was able to finance a larger proportion of its national wealth during World War II and yet maintain interest rates at very low levels? Is it true that after every major previous war, the country has reverted to a gold standard in order to stabilize long-term rate markets and reduce the cost of the overhanging national debt?

4. With some commodity prices now rising and the stock and bond markets in a period of stagnation, are we seeing the beginning of stagflation here? What evidence do we have that the economy is going to grow in any meaningful sense, short of a small bubble that may be simply the result of buyers anticipating future price rises?

5. Mr. Greenspan, on the Senate side you mentioned that the country had 100 year bonds at the turn of the century, and these bonds had very low interest rates. Was this in effect the direct result of a gold standard? If so, what would be the down side of returning to a gold standard, particularly when the current Administration was boasting that its effectiveness (until early this year) was measured by the dropping long bond rates?

6. Apparently, the proportion of health costs paid by the U.S. government has been growing steadily since the early 1960s, from about 20% of total costs to about 50% today. The percent paid directly by consumers, who are the only players immediately sensitive to cost savings, has declined from 60% to 20%. During this time we have seen a steady rise in health costs. Is there a connection, and if so, does the current Administration bill presage higher or lower health care costs from your viewpoint?

BOARD OF GOVERNORS
OF THE
FEDERAL RESERVE SYSTEM
WASHINGTON, D. C. 20551

ALAN GREENSPAN
CHAIRMAN

September 9, 1994

The Honorable Paul E. Kanjorski
Chairman
Subcommittee on Economic Growth
and Credit Formation
Committee on Banking, Finance
and Urban Affairs
House of Representatives
Washington, D.C. 20515

Dear Mr. Chairman:

Thank you for your letter of August 11 enclosing follow-up questions to the July 22, 1994, hearing on the conduct of monetary policy.

Enclosed are my responses to your questions and to those of Congressman Ridge for inclusion in the hearing record.

Sincerely,

Enclosures

CHAIRMAN PAUL E. KANJORSKI
QUESTIONS FOR THE RECORD FOR CHAIRMAN GREENSPAN
HEARING ON FED'S CONDUCT OF MONETARY POLICY
JULY 22, 1994

1. Recent concerns, regarding unprecedented stock market instability, the falling value of the dollar in the international currency markets, and the sustained high level of long-term rates, have raised different questions in regard to monetary intervention by the Federal Reserve. Particularly, in regard to the value of the dollar, in testimony you delivered on Friday, July 15, before the Bipartisan Commission on Entitlement and Tax Reform, you stated that the "U.S. economy has recently been experiencing the ideal combination of rising activity, falling unemployment, and slowing inflation." Yet in your testimony before the Senate on Wednesday, July 20, in addressing the falling value of the dollar, you stated that "the weak value of the dollar internationally is often indicative of possible domestic inflationary evidence" and is generally considered as bad for the economy. The value of the dollar in foreign markets has in fact fallen 5% since you testified before the Senate Banking Committee on May 27, and many have been expecting the Fed to raise rates as the most traditional way of defending a currency. You mentioned to the Subcommittee that you see the decline in the dollar as resulting from buying and selling trends for currency in foreign markets rather than from domestic inflation pressures. At what point would you consider the falling value of the dollar to be severe enough in nature to warrant Fed intervention regardless of the reasons for the dollar's decline, and do you see the dollar as at all mitigating the positive statements you had about the state of the U.S. economy at the Bipartisan Commission hearings?

There is no predetermined extent or speed of decline in the dollar's foreign exchange value that might prompt the U.S. monetary authorities (Treasury and Federal Reserve) to intervene in foreign exchange markets. Such decisions depend very importantly on the surrounding circumstances: Are exchange markets extremely disorderly? Does the dollar's decline seem to be having important spillover effects on U.S. financial markets? Is the dollar's decline severe enough to materially threaten progress toward price stability? Would intervention seem to have a chance of being effective?

Part of the reason for the dollar's decline in the first half of this year was the unexpected signs of stronger growth abroad and the associated implications for foreign interest rates. Nevertheless, the dollar's weakness was troubling on at least two counts--it may have signalled market concerns that U.S. monetary policy tightening thus far had not been enough to forestall a pickup in inflation, or, apart from market expectations, the decline in the dollar itself could have undesirable effects on the U.S. price level, whether directly through the price of imports or, indirectly, through a boost to aggregate demand at a time when the U.S. economy was nearing potential. Thus, U.S. monetary authorities did intervene on several occasions, and we were pleased that the dollar seemed to stabilize after mid-July.

2. Although the nation continues to experience an economic recovery, there is evidence that this recent prosperity may not be widely dispersed. Despite strong GDP numbers and vigorous manufacturing productivity, wages have remained flat. For the roughly 6% of Americans who remain unemployed, job prospects for those at the low end of the skill level and wage spectrum are increasingly bleak. Is there a role for monetary policy to play in alleviating this disparity, or as you suggested in your testimony before the Bipartisan Commission, in reaching this segment of the unemployed population, should we be concentrating on worker retraining and programmatic changes which connect dislocated workers with pockets of the job market in need of qualified workers? In addition, as these goals closely mirror the intent of H.R. 4040, the Reemployment Act of 1994, do you believe that the enactment of this legislation is desirable in order to alleviate the disparity which currently exists? Will enactment of retraining and reemployment legislation help to achieve the mandate of the "Humphrey-Hawkins" Act to secure "the right of every American to full opportunity for useful employment at fair compensation?"

The labor market problems to which you refer cannot be effectively addressed through monetary policy. We do need to focus on other instruments of public policy to deal with the structural unemployment and low real wages that afflict too many in our country. H.R. 4040 is intended to make a contribution by improving the nation's systems for assisting workers who lose their jobs, by integrating a variety of income support, training, and job-matching programs. I am not in a position to offer a judgment on the likely efficiency and effectiveness of the proposed system, which would require a detailed examination of the experience with a variety of programs that have existed over the years. Undoubtedly, many insights in that regard will surface during hearings on the bill.

3. Under the mandate of the Full Employment and Balanced Growth Act of 1978, a principle portion of your monetary policy report must contain a discussion of changes in the monetary aggregates and their relevance to the state of the economy. In the last ten to fifteen years, as you have often noted, the propensity for the aggregates, in particular M2, to meet their targets as outlined by the Fed has been infrequent. Many economists, including Mr. Geoffrey Moore at Columbia University, with whose work you are no doubt familiar, have attempted to include measures on non-monetary financial instruments in explaining the divergence of the monetary aggregates from their targets. Has the Federal Reserve continued to review such new modeling techniques and have they been useful in explaining why the aggregates have been declining in relevance for overall economic forecasting? If other

non-monetary financial instruments are more meaningful indicators, what are they? Do you believe that the price of gold is a more reliable indicator for economic analyses?

The relationship of M2 to the economy has been changing, and as a consequence the Federal Reserve has de-emphasized this variable in making its monetary policy decisions. Because of these changes, there have been times when the Federal Reserve judged that fostering good performance of the economy required that M2 grow outside our preannounced ranges. As you note, an important reason for the anomalous behavior of M2 appears to be the greater variety and easier availability of non-monetary financial instruments, and we have emphasized this in our research efforts. For example, a study by two members of our staff, Feinman and Porter, which was published in September 1992, tested whether changes in the demand and supply of M2 could be explained by including returns on a very wide variety of alternative uses of funds, including intermediate-term Treasury securities and the cost of consumer debt (reasoning that one use for M2 is to pay down high cost debt). Another staff study--by Orphanides, Reid and Small published in December 1993--looked at the influence of stock and bond mutual funds on the public's holdings of M2. Both of these studies had some, but limited, success; questions about the behavior of M2 persist, and we are continuing to research the properties of this monetary aggregate.

In our policymaking, we look at the prices and quantities of a number of non-monetary financial instruments. Among these, some Federal Reserve officials have found the price of gold to be useful for reading market participants' expectations of inflation.

4. The press release on the money supply issued by the Federal Reserve on July 21 showed that the growth rate in the monetary aggregate M2 for the three months ending in June, 1994 was zero. The smaller monetary aggregate, M1, has decelerated rapidly from its much higher growth rates last year to 1.6 percent in the last three months. Some experts, such as Dr. Anna Schwartz, predict that a continuation of this kind of slow or zero money growth could result in a recession. Would you please comment on the implications of this slow money growth.

As noted in the previous question, the relationship of money to the economy has been shifting in recent years. M1 has become much more sensitive to movements in interest rates, obscuring its relationship to current and future economic activity or prices; M2 velocity has behaved anomalously as households take advantage of a wider variety of savings instruments.

As a consequence, double-digit growth in M1 in 1992 and 1993 did not mean that inflation was taking off, and slow growth this year does not imply recession. Moreover, sluggish M2 in 1992 and 1993 was compatible with a strengthening economic expansion. As noted in our report to Congress, the Federal Reserve expects the expansion of M2 to remain damped, and modest M1 growth also would not be surprising, given the rise in interest rates this year. The Federal Reserve will continue to monitor the behavior of money and credit as it seeks to foster sustainable economic expansion. Looking at these variables in the context of a wide variety of other economic and financial data, the members of the Federal Open Market Committee projected continued economic expansion over the balance of 1994 and in 1995.

5. Many economists and analysts have been puzzled by the present levels for the price of gold which have not reached the psychologically "magic level" of $400 per ounce even though recent market tendencies such as flaccid bond values and a decrease in investor confidence would normally have caused an increase to this level. Over the past decade in particular, the international currency markets have become increasingly intertwined with activity in non-monetary markets, in particular that for gold. Do you believe that it is within the mandate of the Federal Reserve System to participate financially in non-monetary markets to more effectively implement or enhance the effect of monetary policy, and if so, under what circumstances?

The Federal Reserve does have the statutory authority to deal in gold, though this authority has not been exercised since the mid-1930s. Unless we are willing to alter a number of institutional arrangements and a tendency toward chronic budget deficits, it is difficult to envision gold playing a central role in monetary policy. Nonetheless, a number of Federal Reserve policymakers, myself included, have found the price of gold to be a useful indicator of inflationary expectations, especially when viewed in the context of other economic and financial indicators.

CONGRESSMAN TOM RIDGE
QUESTIONS FOR THE RECORD FOR CHAIRMAN GREENSPAN
HEARING ON FED'S CONDUCT OF MONETARY POLICY
JULY 22, 1994

1. Mr. Chairman, have the monetary aggregates lost all significance to the point where we should transition to a gold-based system?

Unless we are willing to alter a number of institutional arrangements and a tendency toward chronic budget deficits, it is difficult to envision gold playing a central role in monetary policy. Nonetheless, a number of Federal Reserve policymakers, myself included, have found the price of gold to be a useful indicator of inflationary expectations, especially when viewed in the context of other economic and financial indicators.

2. Is a return to the $350 gold price range desirable, and if so, why haven't the recent interest rate raises been successful in returning gold to this level?

The recent increases in the price of gold may have been associated in part with some deterioration in inflationary expectations, despite the increase in interest rates. Such a deterioration might reflect concerns about pressures on available resources and potential inflationary credit expansions in light of sustained strength in the economy.

3. How is it that this country was able to finance a larger proportion of its national wealth during World War II and yet maintain interest rates at very low levels. Is it true that after every major previous war, the country has reverted to a gold standard in order to stabilize long-term rate markets and reduce the cost of the overhanging national debt?

During World War II, the Federal Reserve supported the price of Treasury debt at artificially high levels (interest rates were held artificially low) to facilitate financing the government's deficit in an emergency situation. The inflationary consequences of this policy were held in check by controls on wages and prices and on credit and by rationing of scarce goods. As controls and rationing were removed after the war, the Federal Reserve had to let interest rates rise to contain inflation.

The historical record of the United States does indicate that policymakers ultimately returned to a gold standard after major wars, which is testimony to the ability of that regime to contain inflation. In such circumstances, market participants are more likely to be confident that inflation would not get out of hand and, therefore, be more willing to purchase a heavy volume of Treasury securities at relatively low nominal interest rates.

As a general rule, the assurance that policymakers seek to foster price stability will be associated with low short- and long-term nominal interest rates.

4. With some commodity prices now rising and the stock and bond markets in a period of stagnation, are we seeing the beginning of stagflation here? What evidence do we have that the economy is going to grow in any meaningful sense, short of a small bubble that may be simply the result of buyers anticipating future price rises?

My assessment of the current economic picture is, I think, considerably more positive than that conveyed by your question. The firmness of consumer sentiment and the deepening order books of U.S. companies bode well for sustained growth of the economy.

5. Mr. Greenspan, on the Senate side you mentioned that the country had 100 year bonds at the turn of the century, and these bonds had very low interest rates. Was this in effect the direct result of a gold standard? If so, what would be the down side of returning to a gold standard, particularly when the current Administration was boasting that its effectiveness (until early this year) was measured by the dropping long bond rates?

As I noted above, the confidence of market participants that inflation will be contained in the future is critical in keeping both short- and long-term nominal interest rates at low levels. For part of the nineteenth and twentieth centuries, the gold standard bolstered that confidence.

6. Apparently, the proportion of health costs paid by the U.S. government has been growing steadily since the early 1960s, from about 20% of total costs to about 50% today. The percent paid directly by consumer, who are the only players immediately sensitive to cost savings, has declined from 60% to 20%. During this time we have seen a steady rise in health costs. Is there a connection, and if so, does the current Administration bill presage higher or lower health care costs from your viewpoint?

I would prefer to defer to those who are more expert in the field of health economics for an assessment of the effects of specific legislative proposals.

O

81-438 (64)